The Life ROI

How to build a strategic plan for life

with your most valuable asset

Jung Park

Photography by Madison Park

Edited by Sarah Soenke

To mom, Alexis, Madison, Mateo, Yeon Jung,
friends, students, and clients. I am grateful for your love, trust, and support.

Table of Contents

Introduction

"Who are you?"

"Who am I?"

Regardless of who is asking, these questions are incredibly difficult to answer. I think it is even more difficult to answer for those of us who are immigrants, bi-racial, or bi-cultural. From my own experience, I have had to continually acknowledge, reflect on, and reconcile my inherited Korean heritage and adopted American culture. Of course, this began when I landed in JFK airport in New York City back on October 21, 1984. Prior to that day, there was no duality in my beliefs, conscience, decisions, or behavior. I am considered to be a 1.5-generation Korean-American. In other words, I arrived in the U.S. when I was in my early teens. The timing of this presents a unique challenge for 1.5-generation immigrants. Naturally, you are already awkward, insecure, and all-around confused as a preteen. But when you take someone that fragile and throw them in a new country where everything is foreign and there isn't a single familiar face outside of your immediate family, then the outcome is traumatic, to say the least. For me, landing in one of the largest cities in the world put extra sandbags on my shoulders as I stood on the starting line of my immigrant life.

By sharing my journey, I hope to shed light on how I arrived at writing this book and why it was my destiny to do this work. In the coming chapters, I completely open myself up and share my deepest inner thoughts, feelings, fears, and love. Some of you may resonate with parts of my journey; for others, my story may come across as fictional. However, I assure you everything that follows actually happened, and I refrained from overdramatizing the events and details. As you read on, I invite you to step into the shoes of a 49-year-old father of two children, husband of 25 years, oldest and only son of Korean immigrants, and older brother of a Korean-American New Yorker. I am also an entrepreneur, strategist, professor, speaker, author, and just another middle-aged human who is seeking answers to the deeper meanings of life. Welcome...

My Journey as: an Immigrant in NYC

The first few years in New York City were all about survival for my family. Prior to our arrival, my father had been working in the United States and saving money to bring the rest of us over. The plan was for him to establish some financial stability before we joined him. However, due to my father's trusting nature and his shady business partner, that plan didn't pan out. My mom brought $2,000 in a traveler's check, and that was all my family had to start our new lives in America. My father found a job in Harlem, working at a fast-food restaurant, and my mom stayed home until she was able to find piecemeal work. As a former pharmacist and real estate developer, my mom must have found it hard as hell to braid neon headbands for a few cents apiece. However, she never showed it. She never complained. As I got older, I realized that my mom is humble and grateful through and through. She never became hung up on her past successes nor allowed ego or entitlement to skew her perspective on the opportunities that came her way. She embraced the opportunity to provide for her family, even if it meant earning a few cents for every neon headband she painstakingly braided. You will learn a lot more about my mom throughout this book as she is my North Star.

While my parents struggled to provide the basic necessities of life for the family, my sister and I were dealing with different struggles. I had completed one semester of seventh grade in Korea, so my parents and I assumed I would be admitted as a seventh grader in junior high school in New York City. That wasn't so. The school administrators told my father that I would need to enroll in elementary school instead. They considered the inability to speak English, as a learning disability. I had to repeat sixth grade again.

P.S. 81 was four blocks from our first apartment in Ridgewood, Queens. Our apartment was on Cypress Avenue, which served as the border between Queens and Brooklyn. We would drive by the school every day. My father would point it out, and I would say I am not going to that school because it looked like a prison. It was a brick building with metal screens on the windows and a fence that wrapped all around the school yard. Portions of the fence were topped with barbed wires. Graffiti covered the building, the yard, and even the fire hydrant in front. This stood in stark contrast to the schools I attended in Korea, and it scared the crap out of me. I was determined not to go to school; in fact, I wanted to go back home. This was not the "America" I thought of when I lived in Korea.

I grew up watching dubbed versions of Eight is Enough, Charlie's Angels, and CHiPs, which were all California-based shows with a whole lot of friendly white people. They featured houses with manicured lawns, palm tree-lined streets, and massive open lanes on the highway. The corner of Palmetto and Cypress in Ridgewood, Queens looked nothing like the images ingrained in my head about "America." Our apartment was right next to the elevated subway track for the M line. There were piles of dog crap, broken bottles, crack pipes, and needles all over the street. In fact, the night my father picked us up from JFK airport in a stinky, beat-up station wagon (he worked in a fish market back then and used his car to pick up and deliver fish), my sister experienced quite a welcome. After my father pulled up in front of our apartment building, my sister got out of the car — wearing her brand-new, black leather, "I am going to America" loafers — and her first step was into a pile of dog crap.

One morning, my father suggested that we go on a tour of P.S. 81. When he saw the look on my face, he quickly assured me that it would just be a tour and, if I still didn't like it, I didn't have to go to school there. Reassured, I went back to stuffing my face. In those days, if I could chew it, I would eat it. I was going through a massive growth spurt, and I would put away an ungodly amount of food at each meal. That particular morning, I was not satisfied with the eggs, toasts, spam (my people love spam, I don't know why), and fruit that my mom served. So, I spread vanilla ice cream over slices of white Wonder Bread and gulfed down half a dozen. After this heart-attack-inducing breakfast, we set out to tour the prison school I had been despising for the past few weeks.

In the school's main office, as my father was talking to a blue-haired lady at the counter, I began to feel my breakfast churning in my stomach, so I squatted behind my father and sister. A few seconds later, my sister released a silent killer that I unknowingly consumed through my mouth during a gravely timed yawn. I thought I was going to throw up all over the office floor. My vision blurred and my head started to spin as I heard my father order me to get up so we could start the tour. My father didn't believe me when I said I had spam and vanilla ice cream threatening to make a reappearance, which had gotten worse from my sister's deadly gift. He thought I was nervous and just wanted to get out of having to tour the school. The blue-haired lady led my father and I to the top floor of the school through a dark, smelly, winding staircase. The lady knocked on a door, which had a small, rectangular glass window with anti-shattering metal mesh inside. The door opened and a giant appeared. She stood 10 feet tall and weighed 1,500 pounds. At least, that is how she seemed to me. She had big blond hair with loose curls and piercing blues eyes. I wanted to turn back and run, but my feet were frozen in place. My father gently nudged me into the classroom. My eyes were fixed on the giant to make sure she wouldn't crush me to death as I stood oblivious to the classroom full of kids. My father and the blue-haired lady shut the door behind me and left. That was my official first day inside the American education system.

In the days, weeks, and months that followed, I experienced many things for the first time in my life. I also learned that the class I was placed in was a special education class. It was a catch-all for students with legitimate learning disabilities, behavioral issues, poor academic performance, and immigrant students. My first reality check came when we went out to the schoolyard after lunch. It seemed identical to any prison documentary where you see the prisoners let out to the fenced-in exercise yard before getting locked up in their cells again. In the midst of kids running, playing, and chatting, a few lunch monitors stood watch to make sure there was no fighting. As the new kid who suffered from a "learning disability," I stood far away in a corner with my back to the brick wall and metal fence. Three boys approached me. The chubby black-haired kid in the middle said something, but my "learning disability" prevented me from understanding. When I stared back at him with a blank look on my face, he pulled out a knife and stuck it against my throat. My "learning disability" did not prevent me from understanding this universal request. I pulled both of my pant pockets inside out to show him that I didn't have any money, then I raised my arms as any proper robbery victim would do. One of the other kids hurriedly pushed my arms down so that the lunch monitors wouldn't see, even though they weren't paying much attention to us anyway. When fear really started to set in, Angel, Pedro, and Eric — three boys from my class — appeared out of nowhere. I had not exchanged a word or even a look with these boys before. They confronted my three bullies. I found out later, from a Korean classmate's translation, that they told the three thugs to back off and that they wouldn't let anyone mess with their classmates. This was sixth-grade territorial tribalism at its best. While Angel, Pedro, and Eric didn't know me from Adam, they were not going to let kids from other classes mess with one of their own.

Blind tribalism saved my butt from three thugs that day and blessed me with three great friends. Angel, Pedro, and Eric took me in. They introduced me to hip-hop, taught me how to breakdance, helped me forge notes to go outside of school during lunch, and made me realize that I was a talented drawer. They constantly asked me to draw break dancers for them and, in return, they taught me graffiti-style drawing and writing. I sincerely believe they planted the seed for my passion for graphic design and typography as we tagged loose leaf papers in those early days.

For the first time in my life, I felt dumb and inadequate. In Korea, I was always within the top 10% of my class. I also served as the class president and vice president from second to sixth grade. In my American sixth-grade class, the only subjects I could participate in were math, art, and gym. I especially thrived in math as the level of math in the Korean education system was a lot higher. Outside of those subjects, I spent the majority of my time looking up every single word in my textbooks. My English-Korean dictionary became my best friend. I was lucky if I could get through a single page while Mrs. Greenburg led the class through entire chapters. To help me with the lessons, Mrs. Greenburg voluntold Hannah to be my translator and peer tutor in class. Hannah and her family were also from Korea and had lived in the U.S. for five years. Her grasp of English was light-years ahead of mine. I was so happy to have a Korean sister in class to help me. Unfortunately, I had yet to find out that Hannah was not happy to be voluntold and had no intention of helping me.

Every Monday, Mrs. Greenburg handed out a list of 20 spelling words that we would be tested on the following Friday. I thought this would be something I could compete on equal footing with my classmates as it only required memorization. I went to work and memorized the crap out of those 20 words. I was so confident that I would get 100%. A rare smile appeared on my face as I thought about how proud my parents would be. Especially because I had only just started school. Unfortunately, I received 60% on my first spelling test. As the test commenced, I started to panic as I could not understand Mrs. Greenburg. Her pronunciation of each word was so different than my broken, fresh-off-the-boat pronunciation! I did my best by guessing which word I thought she was saying. Additionally, my cursive handwriting was way off. While in my view, some of the words were spelled perfectly, Mrs. Greenburg could not read or recognize the letters in my cursive. I was disappointed.

The following Monday, when we received a brand-new list of words, I asked Hannah to read each word out loud while I recorded it on my Walkman. (For those who may not be familiar, this is a personal cassette tape player that could also record audio, much bigger than an iPod) She said it was a stupid idea and she was too busy with her studying to help me. As Hannah turned her back, a friendly face peeked behind her. Lorena had reddish blond hair that was usually braided in pig tails and had freckles on her nose and cheeks. Her family was from Argentina, and while she was born in the U.S., she was fluent in both English and Spanish. It looked like Lorena was asking Hannah about what I was talking about. I saw the universal sign of dismissal from Hannah as she waved her hand in the air. Lorena peeked around Hannah's head, pointed to the Walkman I was holding, and then back at herself. With a simple gesture of her index finger, I found my new peer tutor and an academic angel. I gratefully accepted her generous offer and we went to work at the back of the classroom. Lorena took her time, slowly and carefully annunciating each word on the list. I ran home and got to work. I unlearned my Korean version of pronunciation as I listened to Lorena's angelic voice, and I traced the proper cursive based on her examples. When Friday came, I was flying high! I was ready to crush it! I was able to understand Mrs. Greenburg clearly as if she was speaking Korean. Repeatedly listening to Lorena's recording worked! I carefully wrote out each word as I had practiced at home with the proper cursive handwriting technique. I felt confident when I handed in my test. I couldn't wait to see the 100% in red color pencil on my test on Monday. I remember how I was giddy all weekend in the anticipation of putting smiles on my parents' faces after they got home from working 18-hour days.

I practically ran to school Monday morning. Instead of the pleasantly surprised and maybe even proud expression I expected from Mrs. Greenburg, she called Hannah and I to the front with rage behind her blue eyes. She pointed at my face as she was talking to Hannah. Her voice was low but stern. Hannah relayed the message to me while Mrs. Greenburg was staring me down. I was reminded of the terror I felt on my first day of school. This time, I was sure Mrs. Greenburg would kill me based on the fury I saw on her face.

"Mrs. Greenburg wants to know why and how you cheated on the spelling test," Hannah relayed. "She said how could you possibly get 100% when you just started school two weeks ago and can't say a single word of English!"

I was dumbfounded. I was crushed. I felt the warm precursory sensations of tears forming in my eyes, until I realized how I could prove my innocence. I told Hannah to ask Mrs. Greenburg to wait one second for me. I ran back to my desk and grabbed the Walkman, worksheet, and pages of practiced spelling I did the week before from my backpack. I showed Mrs. Greenburg the workbooks and pages. Then I re-winded the tape and played Lorena's recording. Mrs. Greenburg's face lit up with a perplexed expression I could not readily understand as a 13-year-old. Mrs. Greenburg leaned back in her chair and gave me a wink of approval accompanied by a smile. I was so relieved!

As I walked back to my seat, Lorena gave me two thumbs up while Hannah seemed disturbed and annoyed. That night, I was able to finally put smiles on my parents' faces. I told them the whole story: Hannah's refusal, Lorena's help, recording each word, cursive practice, Mrs. Greenburg's accusation and approval, all of it! My parents came home soaked in grease, sweat, and fatigue that night, but I was able to validate their sacrifice and provide them with a bit of hope and pride. The smiles on their faces inspired and motivated me to get my hustle on. Getting good grades back home in Korea never felt like this. It meant more now; it wasn't just about me anymore. It was larger than just good grades. It was about validating my parents' sacrifice, making the best of the opportunities I was given, and recharging my parents with pride so they can push through another 18-hour workday. They would endure tens of thousands of 18-hour workdays for me and my sister in the years to come.

In the warm days of late April, my entire sixth-grade class was busy preparing for the annual dance festival in May. Each class chose a dance style, all the students had to learn that dance style, and perform it in front of the whole school. For some reason, my class chose country dancing — the two-step to be precise. I was the oldest and tallest in the class, so I was matched up with a Yugoslavian girl named Rose. She was a sweet girl but often was made fun of by some of the boys. John was friends with the crew I hung out with. He was quick-witted and was quick on the trigger with jokes. He loved to poke fun at people, including Rose. As the dance partner of Rose, I somehow became the target of his jokes, too.

During dance practice, we would push all the desks up to the front of the classroom so we could have space to dance. One day, John was not practicing; instead, he was sitting on one of the desks up front, taking verbal shots at his victims as they awkwardly practiced their two-step. Rose and I had our arms around each other's waist, and we were stumbling through our steps when John started up on Rose and me. I kept shooting him warning looks to no avail. I even placed my index finger against my lips to hush John. Nothing worked. John was on a roll. I cannot remember the few seconds right before the incident. All I can recall is getting mad at John to a level where I had tunnel vision and at the end of that tunnel was John's face. Before the music started up again, I ran towards John and delivered a flying double side kick to his face.

My foot slammed him into the blackboard. John clutched his face and curled up. I began punching him while repeatedly screaming "Said Stop!" Some of the boys stepped in and peeled me off of John. Mrs. Greenburg grabbed John by the arm and dragged him out into the hallway while he was sobbing. The door shut, and that's when I started to panic. What the hell did I just do? Am I going to get expelled? No, I am going to get arrested, I just committed an assault! I am going to get deported! Holy crap, my whole family is going to get deported! All because of me.

These thoughts were flashing through my head at 1,000 miles an hour. The door opened and John walked slowly back into the classroom, still sobbing. Behind him, Mrs. Greenburg motioned for me and Hannah to join her in the hallway. I was terrified. As I followed Hannah out to the hallway, I began to sob too. Mrs. Greenburg started talking but with a surprising tone. I expected the same tone as the one she used when she thought I had cheated on the spelling test. Instead, she spoke calmly and comfortingly.

"Hannah, tell Jung that John has been disruptive all day, especially since we started dance practice. No matter what I said, he wouldn't shut up. I also know he was picking on you the whole time," Turning to me, Mrs. Greenburg said, "I would like to thank you for shutting him up. Finally, we will now be able to finish practice in peace. Thank you, Jung."

I recognized the words "thank you" in her sentence and turned to Hannah for clarification. I was new to American culture but even to me this seemed odd. A teacher thanking a student for beating up another student in class? Hannah translated Mrs. Greenburg's appreciation in a tone of confusion. When I looked back at Mrs. Greenburg, she wiped my tears, padded me on my shoulder, and put her index finger up to her lips and winked to convey the secret nature of this conversation. She turned to Hannah and did the same. I was thoroughly confused but relieved that I wasn't getting my family deported. The next day, John and I shook hands and became closer friends. It is always amusing how I have become friends with people I fought or argued with over the years.

A month later, as the sixth graders were counting down the days until graduation, a student committee was formed to prepare for the upcoming ceremony. Teachers nominated students from their classes to join this committee. I, the foreign kid who suffered from a "learning disability," did not expect to join this committee. Frankly, I didn't even know such committee existed until Mrs. Greenburg walked me into the room and put me in charge of the decoration sub-committee. She told everyone that I was the best artist and, therefore, I should lead the decoration efforts. When Hannah translated what Mrs. Greenburg had announced, Mrs. Greenburg gave me her patented wink, which instantly gave me a surge of confidence. For the next few weeks, I led a handful of students on creating decorations and large posters based on the theme "We Are the World" (inspired by the song of the same name written by Michael Jackson and Lionel Richie and produced by Quincy Jones and Michael Omartian in 1985). I had never done anything like this before, not even when I served as class president in Korea. I had to figure things out as I went and quickly think on my feet. I used my hands, body language, facial expressions, and quick thumbnail sketches (before I knew what thumbnail sketches were) to communicate with my fellow sub-committee members. By the end, our sub-committee kicked butt and the auditorium looked fantastic!

At my second elementary school graduation, I was able to make my parents smile again, this time because of a completely unexpected reason. Based on GPA, students from each class were called to the podium to receive small, gold-plated pins for their accomplishments. I expected to receive pins for math, art, and gym, which I did. However, after the pin ceremony, the principal called me up to the podium. I thought I misheard someone else's name and just sat in my chair. After the principal called my name a few more times, my classmates next to me nudged me to get up. Reluctant and confused, I walked towards the podium. Mrs. Greenburg was standing next to the principal. She had the biggest smile on her face. A smile I hadn't seen the entire school year. The principal read from a large piece of paper before handing it to me. I briefly looked down at the paper and did not understand a single word on it. The only thing I recognized was my name. As I stood there still confused, Mrs. Greenburg came around from the podium and gave me a gigantic hug. On my first day of school, I was fearful of this giant. On my last day of school, I was swallowed up in her arms in a warm hug and I felt loved. As I walked back to my seat, I shrugged my shoulders at my equally confused parents to confirm our shared disbelief. When I looked back at Mrs. Greenburg now standing by our class, she gave me her patented wink. It is amazing how such a simple act of an eyelid can lift up a boy's confidence and spirit. As an adult, I am still awed by the power of simple gestures when they come from genuine love and trust. I try to practice this important lesson and invaluable gift from Mrs. Greenburg in my daily interactions with my children and students. Later, I found out that the large piece of paper was leadership award that was given to one student from the entire graduating class each year. I also learned that the incident with John, my work in leading the decoration sub-committee, and Mrs. Greenburg's firm recommendation contributed to this foreign kid with a "learning disability" receiving such prestigious award. I wish I can give a wink of gratitude and respect to Mrs. Greenburg right now.

Mrs. Greenburg's support for me didn't end at graduation. She recommended that I be placed in one of the three honors classes in 7th grade. At first, I was upset and scared about being placed in such an advanced class when I could barely read half of a page in a textbook. I considered asking to be placed in a regular class, but my mom talked me into giving it a try. She reminded me how much trust and confidence Mrs. Greenburg's recommendation showed. I didn't want to disrespect her or let her down. But the learning curve in an honors class was steep. None of my friends from sixth grade was in my class. I had to start all over again. I had to wake up 2-3 hours before school started. I had to look up every word I didn't know from the chapters we planned to go over in class that day. I had to do this type of prep work every day either in the morning before class started or after school.

Otherwise, I could not compete with my classmates on an even playing field. If I wasn't prepared, I would start my school day with a negative balance. It was hard enough to compete as a recent immigrant; I didn't need to start yards behind the starting line every day. I am not the most competitive person, but I do not enjoy losing, especially when it is an away game and I have to fight through opponents, the crowd, and sometimes the referees, too. I truly believe I inherited the traits for hustle and grit from my mom. I was blessed to have these traits during my first few years in the U.S., and I have been steadily building them up over the last 35 years. All that early prep work became simply how I approached every consulting engagement, project, class, and opportunity. I conduct thorough discovery, research, and preparatory steps in all that I do. I want to make sure I give myself the best starting chance each and every time. My philosophy and behaviors which define who I am today were formed in those early years as a 1.5-generation immigrant. As painful as they were sometimes, I am grateful for my 35-year immigrant journey in the U.S.

My Journey: as a Teenager and Young Adult

When I was in seventh grade, I learned from a family friend about the specialized high schools in New York City. At the time, there were four specialized high schools; three of them focused on traditional academics (Stuyvesant High School, The Bronx High School of Science, and Brooklyn Technical High School). The fourth, Fiorello H. LaGuardia High School, stood out to me because it focused on the arts. I also found out that people called this school the "Fame" school because there was a movie and a TV show based on the school. I was sold! Unlike most Korean parents, my mom was supportive of me attending the "Fame" school. Stereotypically, most Korean parents wanted their children to attend one of the three specialized high schools focused on math and science.

My mom had a lot of passion and talent for visual arts and literature. She aspired to paint and write poetry. However, due to financial reasons, her passion had to take a backseat to a practical, stable career. When she was growing up, as the oldest daughter of five, it was difficult for her to attend college. In those days, the norm was for women to stay home and take care of children, and education was reserved for men. My grandfather did not agree with this misogynistic standard and encouraged all four of his daughters to pursue higher education. However, just 10 years out from the Korean War, the Korean economy was in its early stages of rebuilding. My grandfather worked hard as a government judicial clerk, but he had a family of seven to support. Unfortunately, he couldn't afford to send all five children to college. My mom keenly understood the situation. The only way she was going to continue her studies was to lock in a full four-year scholarship. My mom maintained a 4.0+ GPA throughout her primary and secondary education. She never missed a single day of school in 13 years. She religiously studied every evening. Often, her mother would scream at her for running up the electricity bill by studying late into the night. When her mother would turn off the lights on her, my mom would take her books and go outside to study under the moonlight. Her tireless efforts enabled her to receive a four-year scholarship from a prominent university. When she thought her struggles were over and could finally pursue her dream of becoming an artist, her father shared a perspective that would drastically change the course of her life. In those days, there were only two majors that would lead college-educated women onto successful careers; primary education and pharmacy. My grandfather spoke to my mom about creating a self-reliant and independent path for herself. He said she should leverage her college education to earn an honest living so she would never have to rely on a man to support her. He wanted all four of his daughters to thrive on their own and not just survive under the oppression of men. It was a cultural norm in those times for women to stay in abusive marriages because they had no education, alternative resources, or means to gain independence. Of course, this wasn't unique to just Korea. This still regrettably goes on all over the world. My mom reluctantly agreed with her father's practical and forward-thinking advice. She decided to go against her talent and passion to pursue pharmacy. Over the next four years, my mom gritted out the pharmacy program to graduate at the top of her class. As I sit here typing these words, I am once again reminded of how difficult it must have been for her. Working toward your passion can be difficult enough but working toward something you are not passionate about and still putting in 150% every single day seems impossible. Ultimately, the decision to become a pharmacist financially paid off for my mom, as she was able to build a successful career.

Thirty years later, when my mom was faced with the same but different conversation with her own child, she told me about her journey and encouraged me to pursue my passion. Of course, as a teenager, I didn't realize how invaluable that conversation was. She had gifted me unconditional love, freedom, and support.

These specialized high schools required applicants to pass an entrance exam and complete a lengthy application process. The three high schools focused on math and science required you to take the PSAT exam. I took it, just to see how I would do. As expected, I didn't do great. Considering I had been in the U.S. for only two years, the score wasn't too bad. I think I could have just squeaked through at Brooklyn Tech, which had the lowest score threshold. However, LaGuardia didn't require a PSAT score. Instead, it required a portfolio of your work, a live audition, and an in-person interview. By the way, this was all before the internet, which meant I had to physically go to the school and gather hard copies of information on the application process. The school was on Upper West Side of Manhattan. From Ridgewood, Queens, I had to take three subway lines, which took an hour and half one way. I didn't care. I was still determined to go. After I submitted the application form, doubts rushed in as I read the requirement details. I didn't know what a portfolio was. When I looked it up, I realized not only I didn't have a body of work to include but also that I couldn't even afford to buy a portfolio case. Even if I could somehow put something together, how would I do the interview? I can barely put a full sentence together. This was not a spelling test that I could prep for and memorize in advance. I had never done an interview. But somehow, I got it together the day before the audition. I drew all night. I had pencils, a few markers, and a watercolor set. I did what I could with what I had. Early in the morning before my audition, I carefully placed the barely dried drawings and paintings into a brown folder and jumped on the L train to head into the city.

Intimidated does not even come close to describing what I felt as I stood in front of the modern and eight-story-tall Fiorello H. LaGuardia High School of Music & Art and Performing Arts. While other kids were chatting it up, I was frozen in place, just like my first day of sixth grade. I thought of Mrs. Greenburg's wink. It warmed me up and I was able to make my way toward the door.

We were led to a large classroom on the eighth floor. There were desks and chairs lined up in a large rectangular formation. In the center of the room was a table with a pile of random stuff that looked amusingly intentional. The first part of the audition was to do a still life drawing. We were supposed to draw the pile of random stuff on the table. This wasn't too bad. Next, a teacher pulled up a chair and sat in the middle of the room. We had to draw her. Luckily, I had a descent angle so I got lucky. While we were drawing, a teacher would pull one student at a time to conduct the portfolio review and interview. When my shoulder was tapped, I think I peed a little in my pants. The inevitable moment of doom came. I had to walk the teacher through my inspiration, creative process, and techniques used for the pieces in my portfolio. A part of me just wanted to fess up and say, "Look lady, I want to come clean. I pulled an all-nighter and put all this crap together just a few hours ago. I am a hack. I don't deserve to be here. I am sorry to waste your time."

But because of my "learning disability," all I could muster was to say, "I sorry. My English no good. So sorry."

The female teacher had a warm disposition that was different from Mrs. Greenburg's but somehow similar. She smiled, nodded, and said "Do your best."

So, I did. I pieced together a few words when I could find them. The kicker was when she asked who was my favorite artist. I had never thought about this. I had gone to The Metropolitan Museum of Art once with my family, but I didn't pay attention to any artists' names or the titles of their paintings. I was screwed. Then, it popped into my head. "Picasso!" I blurted out.

I had once seen a magazine ad with one of his paintings and his name before. I thought I was saved, but then came the follow-up question, "Why is he your favorite artist?"

Damn it! I didn't have any artistic words in my vocabulary. I only knew one art-related word so I said it: "Color."

I am sure it was absolutely the worst interview that teacher had ever facilitated. I went home after a long day. The 90-minute subway ride home was brutal as impostor-syndrome propaganda filled my thoughts. Sulking and moping ensued in the weeks that followed. When spring came around, I received a letter from LaGuardia. I don't think I had ever been so nervous about opening a letter as I did that day. I quickly scanned the letter for key words like "congratulations" or "accepted." When I found them, I was ecstatic! It didn't seem real. It didn't seem possible. How could I have gotten in? How could they let me in?

It didn't matter. I was in. It was in writing. I couldn't wait to show my parents the letter that night. I was sure this was going to put even bigger smiles on their faces, especially my mom's. And it did. I was so happy. I felt extremely proud. I scored a goal, even though my starting line was behind others', I didn't have the proper gear, and the crowd was booing me. But through it all, I scored. I won.

The educational experience I had at LaGuardia was worthy of the school's nickname. There were five majors to choose from: visual arts, vocal music, instrumental music, dance, and drama. Students attended traditional academic classes in the morning and then attended specialized classes based on their program after lunch. I had the opportunity to explore various visual arts classes: watercolor, life drawing, pen and ink, oil paint, sculpture, photography, art history, fashion design, and graphic design. My world began to grow academically, socially, culturally, and professionally. My family moved to Brooklyn during my freshman year, so I took the F train and had only one transfer to get to school. My commute shortened to an hour. I met kids from all different races, cultures, socioeconomic statuses, and family backgrounds.

I also began working outside of my parents' business. I wanted to independently generate my own income. At the very least, I wanted to be able to make my own spending decisions. The most difficult but financially rewarding job I had during this time was at a fruit and vegetable market. One of my parents' friends owned it. It was in Woodhaven, Queens. I would take three subway lines to get there: F, A, and J. The commute took an hour and half each way. I worked six days a week, from 7 a.m. to 8 p.m. I only had 10 minutes to eat breakfast and 20 minutes to eat lunch. The manager didn't like me. He had a son my age and whatever comparison he was doing in his head was not healthy. He also disapproved of my appearance. I was neck-deep in heavy metal those days. My hair was long, my jeans were ripped (intentionally, which he absolutely despised), and I wore concert t-shirts with satanic-looking band members. He was also a devoted Christian and probably thought I was a devil worshiper.

It was back-breaking work. I would first stack the hand cart with new inventory from the owner's van after he returned from the wholesale market. Then I would organize containers of vegetables and fruits inside the walk-in refrigerator every day to make sure the older inventory was in the font and newer shipments were in the back. It was a small space, and the boxes, crates, bushels, and sacks were stacked from floor to ceiling. It was the worst game of Tetris you could ever play. Each morning, I would bring the display tables out to the street and stack them with fruits and vegetables. I then brought it all back in when closing. Cutting rotten parts off, cleaning, slicing, and packaging vegetables and fruits filled up the rest of the day. I worked my butt off. It was dirty work. I smelled like whatever rotten vegetables or fruits I had handled that day when I returned home. For all this, I was paid $200 a week in cold, hard cash! This was the highest paying, honest job I could get as a high school student. Of course, there were other jobs that offered a lot more cash, but I wouldn't last long in prison, so I was happy to keep the same job for two more summers in high school. I made good money, and I spent it well. I treated myself with fringed leather jackets, Levi's 501s (only to bleach and rip them up), Doc Martens, and all the skull earrings and chains I could wear. I upgraded my Walkman to smaller models with silly features like auto reverse. I was selfish with my money. I bought a couple of bottles of Pepsi for my parents and absolutely nothing for my sister. I was a miserably selfish teenage douchebag. My sincere but terribly delayed apologies to my family!

In my junior year of high school, slowly but surely, I began thinking about what I wanted to study in college and pursue as a professional career. Without much effort, I excelled in my graphic design class. We worked on various projects, from print ads and logos to magazine layouts. I remember one day my teacher pulled me aside to let me know that I was doing a great job and that I should pursue graphic design as a career. He also recommended that I attend Parsons School of Design, if I was interested. After researching the top universities for graphic design programs, I thought Boston University would be a fun choice for me. I wanted to live on my own and experience typical "college" life. Boston wasn't too far from home, so I thought it would be the perfect place. After sharing my thoughts and plans with my parents, I was faced with a reality check similar to the one my mom had 30 years before.

As the eldest son of an immigrant Korean family, it just wasn't feasible for me to attend college in another state away from my family. My sister and I were the only two employees of my parents' business. During the school year, we worked after class and on weekends to help out. My sister and I peeled shrimp, quartered chickens, tended the frying stations, took customer orders, and performed cashier duties. I must admit, my sister helped them out more than me because I did everything I could to get out of working in the restaurant. However, I dealt with the government agencies, utility companies, vendors, and other external entities that required some form of English communication. My father had an adequate working knowledge of English but still asked me to handle things. Maybe he did this so I could practice my English, but he also probably didn't want to deal with the hassle. Either way, my parents simply could not afford to hire other employees. Their small mom-and-pop business brought in just enough to support our family of four and not much more.

The college discussion with my parents was mostly about the cost. Up until that point, I had no idea how much college tuition costs, not to mention room and board, books, food, living expenses, and other fees. I had to forget about Boston University and look in New York City. Luckily for me, the city had no shortage of great design schools. That's when I remembered Parsons School of Design. My parents came up with some magical funding strategies, and I was able to apply and get accepted. Because Parsons was in Manhattan, I could live at home and commute. It was certainly a "privileged problem" to settle for Parsons. I didn't complain back then, and I certainly am not complaining now. I was blessed to have parents who were supportive of me attending college in pursuit of my passion. My mom also gave me a piece of advice that would prove to be true years later: "When you choose a profession that is based on your passion, there might come a time when you end up hating your passion because you have to make a living from it. Making a living means that you have to do things you don't necessarily like to do. If you have to compromise your passion because you are using it to earn a paycheck, you may find yourself severely conflicted."

I didn't quite understand what she meant at the time, but exactly 10 years later, I found myself severely conflicted and have grown to resent my passion for creative work. As always, my mom was right.

On a sunny spring day in 1992, my parents began their day at the restaurant on Flatbush Avenue like any other day. My mom was busy getting ready in the kitchen while my father was setting up the cash register and turning on the fryers. This particular morning, they had a visitor. The bell on the front door jingled as it swung open. Without looking up, my father said, "We are not open yet."

By the time he did look up, the muzzle of a pistol met his forehead. The intruder told my father to empty the register. As he shoved cash into his pockets and kept the pistol fixed to my father's head, my mom peeked out from the kitchen. Fortunately, she remained quiet and ran to the back to hide their additional cash. The robber vanished just as quickly as he had appeared. My parents were blessed that day to only lose their money. Many similar stories do not end this way. It still boggles my mind how calm and collected my parents had been. My father was staring right into the barrel of the gun. The slightest movement, intentional or unintentional, could have ended his life in an instant. According to my mom, he didn't even shake as he emptied the register. He maintained a calm demeanor throughout the whole ordeal. My mom, who typically jumps out of her seat at any loud noise, was pragmatic and collected. Later, my mom correlated my father's reaction to his years of service in the military. My father had served in the Vietnam War from when I was a few months old until I was 2. My mom, who survived the Korean War as a toddler, also was wired to react in the same way. She survived unimaginable hardships during her early childhood years. I come from two mentally tough people. I am blessed.

When the robbery became last month's news, my mom announced to my sister and I that they were going to sell the restaurant and look for different opportunities. It turns out that wasn't the first robbery my father had survived; it just happened to be the only one my mom witnessed. They discussed whether they wanted to continue on with the restaurant after the robbery. My mom told my father, "There has to be other ways for us to achieve our American dream."

My parents sold the restaurant to one of their vendors, and they finally took a much-deserved break. My father lounged around, read, and watched TV. My mom cleaned and rearranged the apartment. She cooked up a storm; even by her standards, she went overboard. When she ran out of things to do around the apartment, she decided to visit her childhood friend in Colorado. Embarrassingly, I had no idea where Colorado was located at the time. Anything west of New Jersey was "the Wild West" to me. My mom spent about a week in Colorado and came back with unexpected excitement. She was convinced that she and my father needed to move there to pursue a new path to the American dream. She didn't pressure us to go with them. In fact, she insisted that my sister and I stay in New York and continue with our studies. By this time, I was finishing up my sophomore year at Parsons and my sister was preparing to start as a freshman. But my parents were clearly concerned about dealing with government regulations, utility companies, and vendors. How would they go about searching for, negotiating, and finalizing business transactions in a new state? I decided to take a year off from school to move out to Colorado with my parents. My plan was to set up their business and return to New York to complete my last two years at Parsons. Typical with most plans, mine didn't play out as expected.

We moved my sister into a one-bedroom apartment in Brooklyn, near one of her close friends. Coincidentally, my parents' friends who ran the vegetable and fruit market, whom I worked for during high school were also heading out west. They, too, had reached their limit for New York City and were ready to find a different path. Their destination was Seattle. We split the U-Haul rental truck and loaded their stuff first then ours. Two Korean immigrant families left

Brooklyn on that hot and muggy summer day. My father and his friend drove the U-Haul and I drove my father's Chevy Lumina with my mom and my father's friend's family. My mom didn't stop sobbing until we reached the Pennsylvania state line. She was heartbroken to leave my sister behind. Now that I am a parent, I can better understand what my mom must have been feeling.

Colorado was a new world to me. Everything seemed so clean, nice, and welcoming. Although I wasn't used to the overwhelming whiteness, I didn't feel scared or threatened. During our first few months, we secured an apartment (the first U.S. apartment I lived in that didn't have roaches or mice), and searched for business opportunities. We visited my mom's friend's liquor store one night, and this black guy nodded "what's up" to me. He was a sight for sore eyes!

Back in New York, my parents' businesses were always located in predominantly black neighborhoods. The financial hardships of immigrant entrepreneurs and of black communities naturally brought these two groups together. The racism my parents typically experienced was offset by good-hearted neighbors who understood we were all trying to survive. My parents didn't drive in from some cushy house in the suburbs to take money out their community. They were just trying to put food on the table like all the other parents in the neighborhood. My father always hired people from the neighborhood for part-time work to help us with cleaning, prep work, security, and other duties at the restaurant. My father made it a point to give back to the neighborhood, and he thought providing jobs was one of the best ways to do so. When I was a teenager, one of my favorite employees was a tall and skinny young man named Keith. He was about 17 years old. Keith worked on busy days: Thursdays, Fridays, and Saturdays. He would help my father clean the restaurant, restock the fridge, and keep an eye out for thieves. The latter was almost a daily occurrence. Inevitably, someone would accuse my parents of not giving the correct change (it was an old trick to pay with a $10 bill and argue that you paid with a $20 bill after the change was given), complain that the ketchup was too watery, or scream, "You are stealing money from our neighborhood, get the fuck out of my country, chink!"

My parents simply smiled and carried on. Keith would sometimes step in if things escalated. Keith genuinely knew and respected my parents as people. My parents treated Keith like the older son they never had.

My 15th birthday was memorable. I wanted to hang out with my friends after school, but my father called to say he was coming to pick me and my sister up. He needed help at the restaurant. I wanted to push back and say, "But it's my birthday! Why can't I stay home and hang with my friends like any other 15-year-old?"

I couldn't say it though. I knew it would be an asshole thing to say, especially since my 12-year-old sister was willing to help. When we arrived at the restaurant, my mom recognized my Resting Mitch Face. (I have been using RMF instead of RBF ever since I realized how gender-biased the term was and I saw a video of a particular joint session of Congress online. Also, I was told Mitch is a good adaptation for the male version of the original "B" word.) She tried to sweet talk me but I was determined to mope and whine. I was standing behind the counter when a boy my age came in and shouted, "Yo, chink! Make some fries and make it fast!"

I dumped a package of fries into the fryer and walked out of the kitchen. I wanted to sulk alone. I had been called "chink" tens of thousands of times by this point. I thought I had developed some callus against the word. For some reason, though, it was different that day; perhaps because I was already feeling sorry for myself for having to work on my birthday. It cut right through me. Keith showed up to work and saw me standing in the corner. He asked me what was wrong, and I didn't answer. I was still busy feeling sorry for myself. After I ignored his repetitive questioning, Keith put his hand on my shoulder and nudged me to turn around. He lowered himself to my eye level and asked me again. I told him, sobbing and slobbering as if it was the worst thing that ever happened to me. I was such a drama king. Keith asked me to describe what the kid looked like. I did, and he told me he'd be back in a little bit. About an hour passed before Keith returned with a firm grip around the neck of the kid who had called me a chink. Keith ordered the kid to apologize to me. With a full grimace, the kid somehow managed to squeeze out the words, "I am sorry."

Keith released him, and the kid stuck his hand out to me. He asked me what my name was. Keith intervened and told him my name was Comet, which was a nickname Keith had given me. We shook hands, and that kid never called me chink again. Keith really took me under his wing. He introduced me to his single mother and siblings. He shared his hip-hop magazines, made me mix tapes, taught me how to properly tie shoelaces, and showed me how to pop and lock. Keith was my brother from another mother.

In the early days of my life in New York City, I had a complicated relationship with black people. For every black person that screamed and cursed at us in my parents' restaurant, there were people like Keith who genuinely embraced and treated us like human beings. I experienced both love and hate. It took me a bit to figure out that there are assholes in every group of people across race, gender, education level, and socioeconomic class.

So, when this black guy nodded to me in Colorado, his gentle eyes and demeanor reminded of Keith. I nodded back. He introduced himself as Chris, which caught me off-guard. I had been in Colorado for a few weeks and was still getting used to random strangers saying hello. The day after I arrived, I went to Subway to get a sandwich. The guy in line in front of me turned and said, "Hey, how are you?"

I looked at him and asked, "Do I know you?"

"Let me guess, you just moved to Colorado?" He replied in disgust. "That's all we need, more assholes like you moving into our beautiful state!"

With that in mind, I decided to respond to this new stranger with my own introduction. After a short exchange about where each of us were from and how we were associated with the liquor store, he asked me if I would want him to show me around town. I said sure, and we exchanged phone numbers. Chris was older than me, married with a son. He instantly treated me like his brother. He brought me over to meet his mom and family. He showed me around town, and I returned the favor in liquid currency.

Despite my parents' genuine efforts during the first six months, every business opportunity kept falling through. When an offer seemed promising, inevitably something would go wrong and the entire deal would fail. In December, my sister came to visit during Parsons' winter break. My parents were seriously considering moving back to Brooklyn in the new year.

Around this time, I was reaping the benefits of all the hard work Chris had put into connecting me with attractive, single women. A month earlier, Chris brought me to a jewelry shop and gallery that had several beautiful girls working there. We went to check it out. He specifically mentioned that I should talk to a certain girl. When we walked in, Chris immediately introduced me to her. After initial pleasantries, I was deeply disappointed with how shallow she was. There were definitely a few cards missing from her deck. As I was trying to graciously wrap up the conversation, Chris was talking to the owner and waved me over. I was saved! He introduced me to the owner, who was a black man from Brooklyn. We hit it off right away and started talking about our home city. As we were talking, I noticed there was a gorgeous young woman with gentle hazel eyes and silky brunette hair eavesdropping on our conversation.

She introduced herself as Alexis. She told me that she had just visited New York with her best friend over the summer. We began chatting about her trip and some of the places she visited that I had also frequented. As we were wrapping up our chat, she asked the same question Chris had asked a few weeks before, "Would you like me to show you around town?"

It is amazing how friendly Coloradans are! I enthusiastically said yes. We exchanged numbers, and Chris and I left (without buying anything, I felt bad for the owner). As we were walking to the car, Chris asked, "You fell for that brunette, didn't ya?"

I shook my head in denial but he saw right through me. "Yeah you did, I can tell! I know that look in your eyes. You done son!"

Chris was right. I called Alexis that night, and we chatted for three hours. Time simply melted away during our conversation. We shared and discovered so many common interests, including our favorite metal band, Mötley Crüe. Alexis invited me to join her and her friends at a local rock/metal club later that week. When I arrived, she warmly introduced me to all of her friends. Then she abruptly left for the bar and made it a point to leave me alone with one of her girlfriends. After few minutes of chatting with the girl I was left with, I excused myself to join Alexis at the bar. Alexis asked me how I liked her friend.

"She seems nice, but all we talked about was cow tipping," I said.

Years later, I interrogated Alexis about leaving me alone with her friend. Alexis never admitted to it, but I am pretty sure it was a test to see if I would just fall a pretty face, regardless of the state of intelligence. We had our first date on a cold January evening, during which Alexis taught me how to drive a manual transmission car (which New Yorkers typically do not drive), a Tex-Mex dinner with potent margaritas, and dessert at a late-night diner. Eight months later, we were married. We have been together for 25 years, and Alexis blessed me with two precious children, Madison and Mateo.

My Journey: as a Professional

When Alexis and I got married in 1994, we were both at the tender age of 23. We were young, naive, and broke but hopelessly in love. During our first year of married life, I worked three different jobs while Alexis continued working at the jewelry shop and gallery. As a young married couple, it was tough to work around the clock to pay the bills while still getting to know each other. It was especially challenging for us because neither of us has ever lived with anyone other than our families. The racial and cultural gap was wider than we expected, but we worked diligently to bridge it. I worked the morning shift at my mom's friend's liquor store six days a week. I worked for a company that painted the interiors of supermarkets while they were closed at night. On weekends, I worked at the same jewelry store and gallery as Alexis. The schedule was brutal, and I couldn't sustain it. After a few weeks, I quit the painting job and took on part-time work cleaning windows and doors at newly built homes. We weren't always able to pay our bills on our own; my parents would sometimes help when we needed it. I knew it would be temporary, though. I had plans to go back to New York City to finish my degree at Parsons and pursue a career in graphic design.

After our first year as a married couple in Colorado, I convinced Alexis to move out with me to New York. Alexis had been attending Arapahoe

Community College, working full time to pay for one class at a time. I loved her independence and drive for education. By this time, my parents owned and operated a deli and grocery store in Irvington, New Jersey, so we discussed living with them while we both finished our degrees. My parents generously agreed to take us in and support us and my sister while we all attended college. Till this day, I do not understand how my parents afforded the house bills, business overhead, and all three of our college tuitions. They worked 16 hours every day of the week for us. To lessen the financial burden and temper my impatience, I took 21 credits a semester to graduate early, held an internship, and helped my parents at the deli on Sundays.

Every Wednesday, I would wake up to go to school, work at my internship, and pull an all-nighter to work on school projects. I couldn't afford to sleep on Wednesdays, I had to grit it out to make sure I was stayed on top of everything. Packing my semesters with the maximum amount of credit hours allowed me to graduate a semester early and save my parents some money. I was able to turn my internship into full-time contract work after I graduated from Parsons. The company was a world-renowned graphic design firm that served Fortune 500 clients. Their work was regularly published in popular graphic design periodicals and won prestigious awards.

Shortly after I started my full-time role, the senior designer I worked under left to start her own design studio. A new senior designer was hired, and she cleaned house. That was the first and only time I was ever fired. It didn't feel good. I grabbed a 40 oz. of Old English and met up with one of my best friends from high school, Alison to vent and sulk. Alison told me about a potential contract position at an ad agency and made an introduction a few days later. The art directors were lovely people, and they loved my work. I started as a freelancer and was able to secure a full-time position after three months.

It was my first official job as a professional graphic designer. The ad agency was Grey Advertising, and I worked as a junior designer for the newly established internet division. I designed first-generation websites for Fortune 500 companies like Procter & Gamble, Hugo Boss, Liz Claiborne, and Lexmark. My team also launched the website for a small, Texas-based, dot-com company called Dell Computers. I had no idea at the time that Dell's revolutionary, demand-generated sales model would impact my own startup venture 10 years later.

About a year into that job, I ran into an ex-employee of Grey Advertising who had joined a smaller dot-com web agency. She told me how much she loved her new job and encouraged me to interview with her company, so I did a couple of weeks later. I met one of the founders and the creative director of the agency. I shared my portfolio and, after a short interview, he offered me the position with a $10,000 salary bump, stock options, and a title promotion to senior designer. I had never negotiated salary before. I'm still not sure where the bravado came from, but I countered their offer by writing down additional $10,000 in salary on a Post-it Note and slid it over to the founder. He had a great poker face. He stared at it for a bit before writing down his response and sliding it back to me. He had crossed off my proposed amount and wrote down $5,000 less. I looked at it and asked, "Is there anything we can do bridge the gap?"

He paused for a moment and scratched his beard. Then he offered me a $5,000 signing bonus that would be paid out over two payments in six months, if my work was satisfactory. Of course, if my work sucked, they could fire me at any time without paying the signing bonus. To be honest, up to this point, I didn't know what a signing bonus was. After the founder explained the terms, I did my best to maintain my RMF and calmly accept the final offer. I did skip all the way back to my office with the biggest Kool-Aid smile on my face though.

When I shared the news with my supervisor at Grey, he told me something I took to heart and promised to practice when I became someone's boss: "As your supervisor, I am going to try my best to get a counter-offer from my boss to match it because I want to keep you here. However, as your friend, I think this offer is amazing and you should take it. It's not just about the salary increase; this offer includes opportunities for you to grow as a professional and advance faster than you could here." I greatly appreciated his transparent response, and I took his friendly advice.

The dot-com web agency I joined, Rare Medium, was founded by three partners who built websites out of an apartment in Manhattan. A few short years later, by the time I joined the company, they had about 60 employees. As a senior designer, I very much enjoyed the increased responsibility and creative freedom. Rare Medium grew like bamboo on a tropical rainforest. Within two years of joining the company, Rare Medium went public and grew from 60 employees in one office in Manhattan to over 1,800 employees around the world. My career grew just as fast. I got to work with more Fortune 500 clients like Forbes, Betty Crocker, Sharp Electronics, New York Life, and J.P. Morgan. I also got to work with multiple innovative dot-com companies that were creating new business concepts and strategies. I thrived working at the breakneck speed. It was the norm for my team to pass around take-out menus around 7 p.m. for dinner and head home around 11 p.m. or midnight. We pulled many all-nighters and often had to wear the same clothes from the day before to client presentations. Spreading ourselves thin over multiple projects was not discouraged. If anything, we foolishly prided ourselves on this unhealthy practice and awarded ourselves with workaholic badges for each sleepless night and every can of Red Bull.

In 2000, Rare Medium landed Corporate Express, an office supply company headquartered in Broomfield, Colorado. This was our first multi-year and multi-million-dollar client, and it brought me back out to Colorado on regular basis. I was selected to lead the user experience and brand strategy portions of the project. I oversaw resources from four different departments in our Dallas and San Antonio offices: usability engineering, information architecture, visual design, and front-end technology. Many of these departments' roles, functions, methodologies, tasks, and deliverables had not existed before. I loved developing and collaborating with colleagues from different disciplines and offices all over the country. I also worked closely with executive level account and project management leaders in Rare Medium. Up to this point, everything I knew about consulting had been self-taught, curated, and made up on the spot. I was exposed to seasoned veterans trained in "The Big Five" agencies. I tried to soak up all of their knowledge, experience, and wisdom every chance I had. Organizationally, I reported up to the Chief Creative Officer back in New York. Functionally, I reported up to two client partners on the Corporate Express engagement team, and one of them was named Bryan Van Dyke. When I began working with this tall, gentle-faced, and reserved Chicagoan, I had no clue he would become such an influential figure in my life. Bryan took me under his wing. He taught, mentored, led, and supported me in ways that all the leadership books preach. He was the walking definition of a servant leader before that was a thing. Bryan was fair, honest, genuine, and likable. It was easy to follow his lead in the office and, just as easily, shoot the shit with him while tossing back some pints after work. Under Bryan's leadership, I felt empowered with the ability to create innovative processes, strategies, and solutions to better serve our clients. I didn't realize until years later that what I was doing was "intrapreneurial". I leveraged Bryan's support and leadership to create innovative solutions that had never been done in the industry before. That experience of autonomy, creativity, and intrapreneurship felt exhilarating and addictive.

Unfortunately, I couldn't avoid the one bad apple in the batch. Based on territorial politics at our Dallas office, a new creative director was sent to Denver to hijack the Corporate Express project. The heads of the Dallas and New York offices hoped I would amicably work with him while they worked out a new organizational structure. This was like sprinkling dirt over a land mine and instructing everyone to simply walk around it and carry on. We had a ton of work to do and we couldn't afford to pause or slow down to deal with this. I remember we had a major presentation for Corporate Express and their global leaders. At this time, Adobe Flash Player was a fairly new technology and was coveted in our industry. Our concept was to build a Flash-based presentation to demonstrate how our solutions would exceed the business, technology, and user requirements. I created a solid strategy in collaboration with the business strategist and technology strategist months before, and Flash was the perfect vehicle to communicate and sell it. When we pitched the initial concept, the CEO and entire executive leadership team expressed their excitement and approval. I went to work with a team in the New York office to create storyboards, scripts, and even an original soundtrack. When a particular leader in our Dallas office heard about it, he insisted that we include his own creative director in Denver. I shared every rational justification for keeping this project within the existing team for consistency and cohesion. I pleaded that this project was way too important and visible to have a new team member join this late in the process. But my efforts were ignored. In defeat, I was forced to include the creative director from Dallas in our process.

In our initial discussion, I asked him about his skill set, knowledge, and preferences to identify which component of the project he should work on. He insisted on creating the Flash presentation. This was the last step of the entire process and the most important part of the project. It consisted of putting together all of the voice recordings, custom graphics, screen mockups, audio tracks, and post-production editing. Naturally, I was very concerned with trusting a new team member with this critical step of the project. Especially someone who thought he deserved my job. The leadership in Dallas insisted on their own creative director taking on the Flash creation assignment.

Reluctantly, I was forced to agree to his assignment due to political pressure. The creative director from Dallas swore up and down about how advanced his

Flash skills were and reassured me that the deadline was more than feasible. The Flash creation began on Friday morning. I was in meetings all day, so I checked in with him in the afternoon. He said he had all the components from New York and had already begun working in Flash. He said that he would work through the weekend to meet the Monday deadline, so I volunteered to work with him. I even bought him breakfast, lunch, and dinner on Saturday. As we worked close to midnight on Saturday, I was concerned about the lack of progress. I asked him if we were still on track for Monday's deadline and, if we weren't, I would start drafting contingency plans. He assured me that we were on track and that the Flash presentation would be done by Sunday afternoon. Against my gut, I told myself to give him a chance.

The next day at lunch, I asked him for a status update and stressed again how important this presentation was for our company. In between bites of cheeseburger and fries, he reassured me that we were good to go. Unfortunately, my knowledge of Flash at this point was novice at best, and I had no way of knowing exactly where we were in the process. I was forced to trust him. Still, I could hear a small voice in my head screaming, "This guy is puttin' one on you. He is taking you for a ride. Do not trust him. You better come up with a back-up plan!"

I decided to listen to my gut this time. I started working on a PowerPoint presentation of carefully sequenced slides designed to mimic our Flash presentation as a backup plan. I had to quickly tell the same story and incorporate the audio files as seamlessly as possible. Around midnight on Sunday, the Dallas creative director came to my cubicle and dropped the bomb.

"Hey bro, I don't think I can get it done tonight," he said nonchalantly. "I'm tired, and I had all these issues with the software."

I had to make sure I was hearing him correctly over the thundering screaming of I told you so! from my gut. With shock, disgust, and terror, I retraced our steps since Friday and counted every time that I had checked in with him. I reminded him of how he had reassured me every time I checked in with him and how there were ample opportunities for him to share the progress with me as I had worked by his side the entire weekend. He simply shrugged it off with a casual, "Hey, shit happens. What can you do? It is what it is."

It took everything in me not to knock that smug look off his face with my knuckles. He said he was going home to sleep and had the balls to ask me what I was going to do. I said I still had a presentation to prepare for the next day.

"What do you mean? You don't know how to work in Flash." he said.

"Don't worry about it," I said as I turned back to my computer. I spent most of that night creating the backup PowerPoint presentation. Before I went home, I emailed my team in New York with detailed instructions on how to sequence the slides and incorporate the audio files. Because the New York office would have a two-hour head start, I thought we could still have the Flash presentation ready in time for the afternoon's meeting. My New York team divided into two groups: one to try to salvage the Flash presentation and the other to finish the PowerPoint presentation. The backup PowerPoint presentation was ready to go by the time I came in the morning. The Flash presentation would take longer to complete. I shared the backup PowerPoint presentation with the US based client members, including the CEO in the morning prep meeting. While the content and messaging were the same, it was painfully obvious to everyone that it was not the Flash presentation I had promised. At the end of the meeting, the CEO motioned me over to share his disappointment and asked me what my plan was for the actual global leadership meeting scheduled in the afternoon. I assured him the Flash presentation would be ready. I was putting my professional and personal integrity on the line. And of course, my job as well.

They had mere hours versus days, but my New York team came through! I was able to download and share the completed Flash presentation at the global leadership meeting in the afternoon. It was a hit!

After the presentation, the CEO came over to me and whispered "That was worth the wait. Good job."

I felt my knees buckle in relief as I thanked him for his patience. As we all headed out to celebrate, I made a stop back at my office. The Dallas creative director was there and had the same smug look on his face from the day before. "How did everything go?" he asked. Oddly, his question came across as rhetorical in tone.

Before I could answer him, he added, "I think I figured out what went wrong with Flash, and I can have it ready for you by tomorrow."

"Nah, we're good." I said before walking him through how I planned for the backup PowerPoint presentation and asked the New York team to complete the Flash presentation. I also shared how it only took six hours for the New York team to complete the Flash presentation. Lastly, I told him what the CEO said after the global leadership meeting and how I was on my way to celebrate over dinner and cocktails with the clients.

"What do you want me to do with my Flash presentation then?" He asked, stunned.

I threw up my right hand and waved him off as I walked out of the office screaming "Fuggettaboit!"

The next day, I reached out to our New York leadership. I painstakingly walked through the past four harrowing days and express my disgust for what had taken place. I also shared my grave concern over what could have happened with our client if the Dallas creative director had his way. A few days later, I received a response saying that the Dallas creative director was reassigned to a "Special project" and would not be a part of my team in Denver going forth. Unfortunately, this would not be the last time I would face personnel issues at work.

I traveled to Denver and Dallas every week until Rare Medium decided to open the Denver office. I was promoted to Director of User Experience in Central Region, which tasked me with relocating resources from our offices in Dallas, San Antonio, Los Angeles, and New York, as well as hiring new employees. The company moved Alexis and I back to Colorado with all expenses paid for and a generous moving stipend. Alexis was thrilled to be back in her home state but I wasn't. I had to leave my parents and sister back in New Jersey, prioritizing my career over my family. This may be the most obvious and natural choice for many people. However, as a 1.5-generation immigrant who had already been uprooted from my extended family, this was quite difficult and traumatic. I have always relied on my immediate family for love, support, and reasons to live. I felt like my guilt weighed heavy enough to prevent my flight from taking off that day in Newark Airport. In some ways, I wished it would. Despite all the love and support from Alexis, I could not stop sobbing. Rather than being excited about my promotion, I was heartbroken over leaving my family. All I could hear in my head was, "You are abandoning them, after all that your parents have sacrificed for you. Who is going to help them now? Mr. Big Shot, it's all about you, isn't it? You're a selfish bastard!"

In the weeks and months that followed, no amount of professional accolades or financial compensations could fill the void in my heart.

Rare Medium was one of many companies in our holding company's portfolio. In 2001, during the dark times of "dot-bomb", our holding company made the decision to shut down Rare Medium on a global scale. However, the Denver office was still servicing Corporate Express and had enough work to sustain our continued operations. Two senior-level client partners including Bryan, two project managers, and I decided to negotiate with our holding company to purchase the Denver office so that we could operate as our own consulting agency. We worked tirelessly to save the jobs of our staff members while we pursued an exciting opportunity to run our own company. I was the least-experienced member of the five partners. I was grateful to be included. Despite all of our efforts, the negotiations fell through and we found ourselves unemployed. The severance package was as bleak as the future. This was not what I had imagined when I left my family in New Jersey to prioritize my career.

Luckily, my parents had decided to sell their business and move Colorado with my sister a few months before I got laid off. By the time I was making weekly calls to the unemployment office, Alexis had started working as a guidance counselor at a high school in Denver Public School system, and my parents had opened a restaurant in Lakewood. I applied to every job posting I could find, followed up on every lead, attended every networking event, and even reached out to former colleagues and partners in New York City. Nothing came through. While job hunting, I hustled as much as I could to generate income. I turned my bathroom into a darkroom, made wooden frames, and silk-screened my own designs onto T-shirts. This was long before on-demand, custom T-shirt websites like eBay, Amazon, or Etsy existed. I designed, printed, packaged, and sold T-shirts at craft fairs. I think I sold three in total. It was a bust. I also used Adobe Illustrator to turn photographs into block-print-like illustrations, which I charged $10 apiece. This was also before all the photo apps with fancy filters that exist today. While it was time-consuming work, my time was free, and every dollar counted.

Alexis's distant family member hired me to paint and tile the doctor's office she worked at in Greely, Colorado, about 80 miles north of where we lived. I loaded up our SUV with supplies, equipment, and tools and headed up with my sister. Our plan was to work through a few weekends, while squeezing in a few catnaps here and there. My sister and I were simply excited for the opportunity to make some cash, regardless of how grueling the work and commute would be. We originally planned to take three weekends to complete the work, but Alexis's family member insisted that we complete the work in two weekends and finish before the New Year.

As my sister and I worked through the night, we realized it would be impossible to finish on time. Alexis and my parents must have read our minds because they drove up on the second Saturday to help us. All five of us gritted through gallons of paint and grout. By that second Sunday evening, we were able to finish the job. It was not our best work, but it was the best we could do under the time constraint. While I was so thankful for Alexis's and my parents' help, I still carry a heavy burden in my heart till this day. Alexis was in her first trimester while she was helping us, breathing in paint fumes, and sleeping on the cold floor of the doctor's reception area. A week later, on New Year's Eve, Alexis experienced excruciating pain in her lower abdomen, and I rushed her to the emergency room. We worked our way through the holiday drunks and were admitted to an examination room. While we waited for what seemed like an eternity, Alexis abruptly got up and ran to the bathroom. She came out a few minutes later with an expression of deep dejection and tears running down her face. Alexis felt our first baby pass through her and out of our lives. When the doctor finally came in, he confirmed our loss. I still remember driving home with Alexis in the passenger seat while the first sunrise of 2002 peeked through the rear-view mirror, obstructing my already tear-blurred vision. While there was no conclusive correlation between Alexis helping us and the miscarriage, I could not help but to blame Alexis's family member whose arbitrary deadline lead to Alexis's involvement. It would take years to resolve my anger towards that family member. However, there is still guilt in my heart.

During those difficult days, I also did all I could to help my parents' restaurant. I visited every nearby car dealership because dealerships often order lunch for their staff on Saturdays. I had never done any sales work before, especially this type of cold sales, but desperate times called for desperate measures. I was willing to do anything and everything to help my parents. I marched in with menus and spoke with anyone who would lead me to the lunch decision maker. I was only able to get a single lunch order from one dealership. It was clear that my sales skills sucked. The only thing that worked, however short-lived, was the email I sent to the food editor at a local newspaper. I wrote about my parents' untimely grand opening the day before the tragic 9-11 in 2001. I wrote about their successful delis and restaurants in New York and New Jersey, their humble start in U.S. as Korean immigrants, and their aspirations of introducing East Coast and multi-ethnic flavors to Lakewood, Colorado. I guess my desperation came through. The food editor came out, interviewed my parents, wrote a heartfelt article, and published it with a great photograph of my parents. After the article came out, my parents saw a rush of customers that they hadn't seen since their Brooklyn days. It looked like luck was finally on our side. Unfortunately, the rush only lasted a couple of days. In hindsight, I think the New York-style deli/cafe concept was ahead of its time for Lakewood in 2001. There are restaurants, delis, and cafes with similar menus now thriving all over the Denver metro area. Timing is everything. This was my mother's first and last failure as an entrepreneur.

Just as my parents were selling their restaurant at a huge loss to another immigrant business owner in 2002, I was able to finally get a job. I was hired by the founder of a corporate branding firm. It was the first time in my career that I would for a private, family owned company. I had no idea what I was getting myself into, but I didn't have any other options. I took a 50% pay cut, but some income was better than none. Every dollar mattered, especially during that time. I didn't have any leverage in this negotiation. This founder knew he had all the cards and I had no choice but to play his hand. I was hired as a project director and was given an office that was once a supply closet. My job description was to serve as the conduit between the strategy and design departments to ensure that our client work was creative, effective, strategic, and cohesive. Additionally, I was tasked with serving as the change agent, which involved creating and implementing change management on process, delivery, and quality of work. One factor that was not clearly communicated to me during the hiring process was that while I would be held accountable for the outcomes, I would have absolutely zero authority to carry out any changes. I found out after I got hired that the founder had "retired" from the management and operations of the firm. His son and son-in-law were supposed to be his successors, and each would manage different functional areas of the firm. On paper, I reported to the son-in-law. However, in his "retirement," the founder still maintained his executive office, kept regular office hours, and made decisions behind his successors' backs, such as hiring me. Within the first week, I was exposed to all the red flags I wish I had seen before.

I had faced racism on a daily basis in New York City. You could say that it was a consistent part of my childhood and young adulthood. I knew what racism sounded like, smelled like, and felt like. But for the first time in my life, I experienced racism that was implicit rather than explicit. I realized that I was used to a kind of in-your-face racism, where you can deal with it head on. I was caught off guard by this new implicit delivery of racism. Sometimes statements seemed innocent, even complimentary at first, but it would inevitably hit me moments or hours later. My inner voice would repeat what the person had said, and I would start to see correlations between these incidents and the explicit hate I had faced back in New York City. The word choice, tone, and facial expressions may have been different, but the core message was the same:

"You don't belong here."

"You are not like us."

"You are not smart enough or good enough."

"Get out."

"Go home, chink!"

When I've shared what my colleagues have said to me at this firm, some people have dismissed their meanings or accused me of being too sensitive. What they failed to understand is that it brings me no joy, satisfaction, or triumph to share these ignorant and hateful statements. I am not using these statements to win sympathy. Everything I share in this book has been said to me — not assumed, not heard through second-hand accounts, not exaggerated or fabricated — but explicitly stated to my face.

A few days after I started, a designer walked in to my closet-turned-office and asked, without any greetings or pleasantries, "Hey, why do you get to have an office when I have been with the company for six years and still have to sit out there in a cubical?"

Before I could process his random question, he carried on, "Are you special or something? You special, ain't you?"

Once again, before I could respond, he answered his own question. "Yeah, you special. You special because you are supposed to be a big shot from New York!"

Ironically, the only prior interaction I had with this man was a brief introduction on my first day. I had yet to have a conversation with him, let alone tell him about my origins. I finally had a chance to respond.

"First, I do not consider this an office, as it used to be and still looks and smells like a closet," I said. "However, if you would like to have it, be my guest. I didn't ask for it. It was given to me, and I do not care whether I work in a cubical or in this closet. Second, why are you in my face demanding answers when I do not have the answers you are looking for? I didn't assign this office to myself. Why don't you go ask the people in charge of making such decisions?" He just stood there with a sour and dumbfounded expression, so I asked him a follow-up question. "Is there anything else I can help you with?"

He left my office without another word. Later on, I found out he was originally from Upstate New York. It is so silly to be that tribal when we're from the same state. He saw me as a stereotype from the Big Apple. According to this image, I am a boastful douchebag who undeservedly goes around taking positions, titles, and offices from hard-working guys like him. Despite my best effort to work with him, he would resist my lead and even sabotage our collective work. This was the second personnel issue I experienced in a professional environment. This designer sat around and surfed the internet for three days while he was supposed to be coming up with concepts for a brochure project. Brochures aren't exactly the most challenging as far as creative work is concerned. He went on and on about all the reasons he didn't have a single viable sketch ready. He recorded three full days of conceptual work on his timesheet, which my budget absorbed. There was an intense internal pressure from management to make sure all projects came in under budget. Although billable hours were often underestimated, the firm remained profitable because the employees were grossly underpaid. There were senior-level designers who had been with the firm for 20 years who were making the same salary that I did as a new hire. Even with the differences in cost of living between New York and Denver, our salaries were way below market. The billable hourly rate was padded to cover overhead and then some. The company had every right to protect its profit margin but not at the expense of its overworked, under-valued, and never-appreciated employees. This designer knew that the quickest way to sabotage me was to falsely bill hours or delay my projects and milk more hours out of the stretched budget. I pulled him into a conference room and gave it to him straight.

"We are both fathers and husbands simply trying to provide for our families," I reminded him. "I do not know why you feel the need to do what you're doing, but it is not helping either of us." He played dumb, so I called him out not only as an ignorant project director, but also as a fellow designer and former creative director who actually developed, implemented, refined, and trained creative methodologies. He didn't have much of a defense.

"In 10 years, you and I will not matter to each other," I said. "We are simply working on this project together temporarily, whether that is for a few months or a couple of years. We do not need to stress each other out like this. The work is difficult enough. We do not need the drama."

I reminded him that I was capable of doing the design work myself and, if he could not conduct himself like a professional, I would be forced to treat him as a junior designer and micro-manage him. I explained to him that I do not enjoy micro-managing but, if forced, I can be very effective at it. "What would you like to do? It's your move."

He did not take responsibility and did not agree to a symbiotic approach going forward. He was a stubborn one. So, I micro-managed him every step of the project, and he asked to be put on another project. You win some, you lose some. Sometimes when you lose the right one, it isn't really a loss.

There was a strategist who specialized in brand research at the firm. He was in his late fifties and had a PhD. I respected his work, approach, and intellect. We were on a business trip together. We had a successful day of meetings with clients and decided to grab some dinner and drinks after work at a local pub. After reflecting on the day, he shared his take on my hiring at the firm.

"I was surprised to see that the firm hired you, especially since the old man (i.e. the founder) hired you," he said. "As long as I have been with this firm, we have only hired junior-level staff, fresh out of school, so we can get them cheap and train them our way. So, I was surprised when someone with your experience was hired."

I thought he was about to compliment my merit, talent, and capability, so I was ready to order another round of drinks.

"Did you know that the old man fought in the Korean War?" he asked. "You know he walks funny because he got shot in the buttocks during the war?"

I didn't expect this turn in our conversation. "Yeah...? And what does that have to do with me getting hired?" I asked in a complete confusion.

"I think he hired you because he feels bad about what he did to your people during the war."

WTF? was ringing loud and clear in my head. "Excuse me?"

I had to ask for clarification as I desperately hoped for a reasonable explanation. "Yeah, I think he feels guilty toward your people, so that's why he hired you."

I was gravely disappointed. I was disappointed that I heard him correctly the first time. I was disappointed that this highly educated and intellectual man could not see past my slanted eyes and what they represented in his ignorant mind. Apparently, my hiring was nothing more than a reparation offering from a Korean War veteran. It had nothing to do with my skills, capability, or talent. It really had nothing to do with ME because he did not recognize me as an individual. I wanted to dump the pint in my hand over his head. But I couldn't. He was much older than I was. I couldn't even slam him through a verbal rebuttal. The only thing I could muster up was, "So, that's what you think, huh?" He was an influential figure at the firm and could easily retaliate. I was powerless. I wanted to stand up to him but I couldn't, not if I wanted to keep my job. Later, I would find out that some of my colleagues and friends also experienced similar incidents. Some of my female colleagues and friends experienced far worse.

I finished my drink and headed to the hotel. I told him I was tired. I wish I could have told him what I was tired of. This was neither the first nor the last incident of racism and prejudice I experienced at this firm. The culture was toxic, and so were some of the people.

The son-in-law I reported to seemed like a stereotypical quarterback: tall, blonde, mustached, and with a shallow charm and intelligence. He would scan through popular business books, articles, and publications for trendy terminologies and acronyms to use in client meetings. These would get him through an initial meeting or two, but any client with substance and experience could see right through him. He would often take credit for the good work of his direct reports and present it as his own. Sometimes, he had the decency to ask to be prepped before the meeting, instead of butchering someone else's work with his own fake dust. One day, he walked into my office to have a chat as I sat in my desk chair. Instead of sitting in the chair opposite my desk like a normal person, he placed his right foot on the empty chair and put both of his elbows on his bended knee. He looked like he was posing for a Marlboro ad. He started talking about an upcoming client presentation and what he needed to know to present my work. He reasoned that due to my Bachelor of Fine Arts (BFA) degree, he could not afford to have me present any strategy or analytical work to clients. He was concerned that they would not trust my presentation because I was a "creative type."

There I thought, So, I'm enough of a "business type" to do the actual strategy and analysis work but I'm too much of a "creative type" to present it?

That's when he straightened up and put both hands inside his baggy, double-pleated, and cuffed trouser pockets. He locked eyes with mine and, as he stood there, started playing a game of chicken and pocket pool (if you don't know what this is, Google it). It was immediately clear to me what he was doing, even though I had never seen someone do it in front of me before. This was a nefarious act of an insecure and toxic leader to establish his supremacy. I was not going to break eye contact and lose to his depraved game. I was not going to give him that satisfaction. If this had taken place anywhere else and he didn't sign my paycheck, I would have immediately put a stop to it. Later, at a happy hour with colleagues, I learned that he did the same thing to a female coworker in her office. She put her head down in shame when she said that she lost the game of chicken. She said she had no idea what he was doing and, before she knew it, it was already too late. I had the displeasure of introducing her to the term "pocket pool." I shared my similar experience, and we consoled each other. To put this incident in context, my colleague was a young woman in her early twenties and the offending executive was in his late forties or early fifties. She was young enough to be his daughter. I sincerely hope his daughter never experiences what he did to his own employees. I sincerely apologize if you have never heard of this game and I introduced it to your vocabulary. I would also like to sincerely apologize if you have experienced someone else playing this game in your presence. I am sorry you just had to relive that. It is quite disturbing to maintain eye contact and a straight face while someone is engaged in a full remodeling project in their pants.

I was determined to stick it out, at least for a year. After all that my family and I had gone through, I desperately needed this job. Also, I thought that any employment lasting less than one year would look like a blemish on my resume (this is a myth). Five months into the job, I experienced my first physically traumatic consequence. I had another long and toxic week at work, and I plopped myself on the couch Friday evening. When the eighth showing of

Sports Center was over, I got up from the couch and felt an excruciating pain on the left side of my neck. I had never felt so much pain in my neck before. My head was also locked in a left-tilted position. When I tried straightening it out, the pain rose to another level. I winced, sat back down on the couch, and decided to wait it out. In less than 30 minutes, the pain spread to my chest, shoulder, and the left side of my back. Not only could I not move my neck but I also could not move my upper torso. I panicked. I told my wife about the pain, and she suggested we go to the emergency room. I stubbornly refused and decided on a more non-medical and familiar treatment of bathing in Epsom Salt. It didn't work. I managed to get a couple of hours of shut eye on the couch and called an acupuncturist that my family had used before. Even though it was the weekend, he agreed to see me. After the examination, he seemed very concerned.

"What did you do to yourself?" he asked.

"Nothing, I just laid on the couch," I said in a childishly defensive tone. "I didn't do anything physical to cause this."

"I mean, what have you been doing that was so stressful that your body broke down like this?" he clarified. "Your body is calling it quits because of the sheer amount of stress your body was forced to endure."

There was only one answer to his question: my job. The daily incidents of disrespect, dismissals, micro aggressions, and other aspects of the toxic culture finally took a toll on my health. I was aware of the harmful effects stress could have on the human body, but I didn't think it would happen to me. I always thought stress was a part of life and you just put up with it. After a lengthy session of needles, I was able to move a bit easier and was sent home. I had multiple follow-up sessions and was put on an herbal medication regimen for months. Eventually, I returned to my normal physical condition, but the mental stress never went away. I stuck it out for seven more months after that to complete a full year of employment. It was a long and painful year. However, looking back, I can confidently say that the level of stress and pain proved to be equivalent to the enlightenment and self-growth that I achieved.

When I left that job, I had a friend who was in the Professional MBA program at the University of Colorado Denver. He spoke very highly of the learning experience, and it seemed to be exactly what I needed in my life. So, I decided to go back to school and get my MBA. I had no idea how drastically the MBA program would change the trajectory of my career and life.

My Journey: as an Entrepreneur

My first semester at the University of Colorado Denver was intimating. As a creative professional with a Bachelor of Fine Arts, I did not feel like I belonged in business school. I felt inadequate and dumb. Once again, my inner voice kicked in and screamed, "You don't belong here. You are not smart enough. You are not good enough. Get out!"

While my impostor syndrome was very active during the entire program, it significantly lowered its volume during one particular semester. I had declared entrepreneurship as my emphasis in the MBA program. Knowing that I come from a long line of innovative, hardworking, and motivated entrepreneurs, I had aspirations of starting my own company someday. I had no idea what type of business I wanted to start or when, but I figured learning about entrepreneurship would help me regardless.

Spring semester of 2004, I enrolled in a class all about writing your own business plan. After learning the required components of a business plan, students had to write a plan either for their own idea or for another entrepreneur who needed help. Based on my experience at the dot-com web agency, I decided to write mine on a Customer Relationship Management (CRM) solution designed to help health and wellness-focused grocery markets. I thought it was an emerging industry with great potential. I recruited the former director of technology from Rare Medium to join me as my partner. My strategy was to have him develop the technical solution while I developed the business model, branding, marketing, and user strategies. The marketing plan was due halfway through the semester, right after spring break. This was a major milestone to gauge the viability of the plan and what refinement may be required. While I was completing the marketing plan, my partner called and said that he wouldn't be able to continue with the project because his work schedule had become too demanding. I completely understood, but I was left with a marketing plan and no product. Even though my professor assured me that it would be ok to complete my business plan on this CRM idea, I didn't want to spend the rest of the semester working on a plan for a fictional technology. It felt like a waste of time. I had roughly two months left in the semester to find a new idea and write a new business plan from scratch. There wasn't any time to waste. I decided to go through an old notebook I used to jot down interesting concepts, crazy ideas, and random doodles. I stopped on a page that had this silly idea my former colleagues and I discussed while having drinks on a typical happy hour on a Friday.

After I had moved to Colorado from New York City in 2000, I found it difficult to get a good haircut. For those of you who may not be aware, Asian hair is quite difficult to cut properly. It is thick, straight, and unable to hide or minimize imperfections, especially for short hairstyles. Based on my own experience, the stylists at upscale salons in Cherry Creek acted as if they were doing me a favor, even though I was paying an arm and a leg for a haircut that was mediocre at best. The franchised salons gave me the worst haircuts ever, which made my head look like a Cuckoo birds' nest. The old-school barbershops made me looked like either an IRS auditor or a newly enlisted army recruit. No disrespect to accountants and service men, but neither were the hair style I was shooting for. When I was working at Rare Medium, I got away with growing my hair out and putting it into a ponytail. Long hair worked in the creative culture of the dot-com world. However, it conflicted with the rigid culture of the corporate branding firm I joined in 2002. I had to cut my hair. I went through months of hassle, frustration, and disappointment in trying to get a decent haircut. Eventually, I had gotten so frustrated that I decided to just shave my head. I bought a $10 clipper at Walmart and shaved my head every week. It was simpler, easier, and definitely cheaper. At that Friday happy hour, I shared my frustration with some colleagues of mine. Apparently, I wasn't alone. Some of my colleagues had similar frustrations. Naturally, as the drinks flowed, so did our entrepreneurial spirits. The conversation led us to start brainstorming alternative solutions. There was no shortage of ideas being tossed around as the night went on. Unlike other far-fetched brainstorms, I actually thought some of the ideas we discussed were viable. So, in my notebook I had written down: Hair salon/barbershop for men, decent haircut at a reasonable cost, beers, sports on TV, T-shirts, socks, hats, etc.

This idea seemed convenient and easy to execute in a business plan. I also figured that if I have to cram a comprehensive business plan in two months, I might as well choose a fun idea. I developed a business model that combined grooming services, retail clothing products, and male-centric amenities in one location. Based on my market research, this was a brand-new concept in Colorado. I had found one similar concept in New York City and Atlanta. Every student in my business planning class had to submit their business plan to the University's annual business plan competition. Without much thought, I submitted mine and went on a trip with my wife to celebrate our 10th wedding anniversary. I completely forgot about the competition during our trip. When we returned and I checked my email, I was surprised see that I was selected as one of six finalists for the competition. Although I was initially excited, panic set in pretty quickly as I read about the rest of the finalists and their business plans. Some of them already had their businesses in operation, had real customers, and revenue. The majority of the finalists had teams of multiple people; only two were single-member teams. All of the other finalists' business concepts provided tangible and significant benefits to their customers and the community: financial planning, bio-tech innovations, retail efficiencies, sound insurance solutions, etc. My concept would help men look prettier. No matter how I looked at the situation, I couldn't help feeling intimated and inadequate. A familiar voice chimed in: Drop out of the business plan competition before you make a fool out of yourself in front of everybody. You don't belong among the finalists; your plan is crap! Maybe they needed to include you because you are an Asian and the school needed to meet some minority quota.

I sure didn't want to make a fool of myself, so I spoke with my professor about pulling out of the competition. His advice was quite direct and effective. He told me that I had a competitive advantage because my business concept was simple and easy to understand. Complexity doesn't necessarily equate to viability. He told me to just have fun with it. While it was impossible to dismiss my anxiety, I did my best to follow my professor's advice. At the time, my wife and I were living in a tiny one-bedroom apartment, my desktop computer was broken, and we were expecting our first child. To say we were financially strapped would be an understatement. I had to create the pitch deck at the university computer lab and borrow a friend's laptop on the day of the actual pitch presentation. I didn't have a suit to wear, so I mixed and matched a jacket and pair of slacks. I was reminded of the night before my audition at La Guardia High School. My preparation was ghetto then, and here I was 20 years later, still in the same mode.

I hitched a ride with a friend to the competition so that my wife could pick up my mom, drive over later in the morning, and we could all drive back home together afterward. I was supposed to present fifth out of the six presenters. This gave me plenty of time to observe the other presentations and prepare how I would meaningfully distinguish my pitch. The majority of the competitors were in formal matching suits. One team had matching polos with their logo embroidered on the chest. When it was close to my turn, I started setting up the laptop on the podium when my wife came up to ask if I needed help. I told her I was good and gave two thumbs up to my mom sitting in the audience. All the while butterflies were engaged in World War 3 in my stomach. As I opened my presentation, I decided to pivot my potential competitive liabilities into intentional competitive strengths. Because all the other competitors wore dark, formal suits as they presented their serious concepts, I decided to lighten up the mood. I wanted to elevate the energy in the room and draw in every audience member. When the event's emcee introduced me at the podium, I intentionally and slowly took my black jacket off as I walked up so that everyone could see it. When I began addressing the audience at the podium, I slowly rolled up my baby blue shirt sleeves. This look, complete with a striped tie and off-white slacks, was definitely more casual and approachable than that of my competition. I started off by asking the audience how they were doing, similar to how a stand-up comic would, instead of jumping straight into my pitch. I began my pitch with carefully planned visual aids and questions to get the audience in the right mindset. I wanted the audience to experience conversational participation. Every one of my jokes was met with louder laughter than I had hoped for. The audience members' head nods of validation were tremendously encouraging. I had never felt this kind of collaborative and synergistic energy before. It felt novel but familiar, comfortable, and yet sharply exhilarating at the same time. Whatever this was, it elevated me to a level I had not thought possible. I was instantly addicted. It wouldn't be until years later that I would realize the depth of my addiction.

After my 30-minute pitch was over, the three judges took 15 minutes for questions. They were venture capitalists, seasoned entrepreneurs, and veteran business professionals. Surprisingly, they didn't have any critical questions or concerns about the viability of my concept or business model. Perhaps my professor was correct. My concept was simple and easy to understand, so there were very few questions from the judges. I felt relieved for both completing the pitch and not being criticized by the judges.

A luncheon followed while the judges sorted out their scores to decide the winners. The fourth-, fifth-, and sixth-place winners would all receive $1,000 in prize money. Third place would win $2,500, second place $5,000, and first place $10,000, along with pro-bono professional services from in-kind sponsors. In my mind, a battle ensued between my newly found voice of confidence and the same-old voice of insecurity, fear, and hate.

"You may win this thing!"

"Are you serious? Give me a break. Did you not hear the other pitches?"

"We did such a great job with the pitch. Did you not notice how engaged and excited the audience was?"

"Fluff. Making people laugh like a clown. You were a joke. You did your song and dance. That's all you did, monkey boy."

I made small talk with the person next to me while trying not to choke on the food I was mindlessly shoveling into my mouth. After a keynote presentation and messages from various school administrators, it was time for the inevitable announcement of the winners. I folded up my napkin and placed it on the table, fully prepared to go up when they called the fourth, fifth, and sixth-place winners. To my surprise, they didn't call my name. They announced the third-place winner, and it wasn't me. I looked over to my mom in dismay. She had lowered her head and was intensely staring at her hands on her lap. I didn't want to make eye contact with anyone because I wasn't sure what I was feeling and I certainly didn't want my RMF to look more awkward than it usually does. I lowered my head as they were about to announce the first-place winner. For that brief moment, the battle in my head stopped. There was actually silence.

Then I heard my business, MetroBoom, and my name. For reasons I couldn't understand, my eyes welled up with tears. I had never cried for joy before. As I stood up, I looked over to my mom. She still had her head down and, without looking up, she calmly said, "Don't get emotional. Stay cool. Do not show your tears."

How did she know? How was she so calm? My wife was not calm at all. She was screaming and jumping up and down. At that moment, I felt deep, genuine love, in two very different ways, from the two most important women in my life. Later, my mom told me that it felt like her heart was about to explode during those moments right before and after the announcement. I asked her how she was able to seemingly remain so calm and why she told me not to show any emotion. She said she didn't know how she managed to stay calm, that it just kicked in. My mom wanted me to display confidence and strength. She wanted me to show that I belonged on that stage as the winner. She said she had no tears of surprise because she knew I deserved to win.

The weeks after the business plan competition were full of congratulatory messages, interviews, articles, and recognitions. I wanted to take my wife to Las Vegas with the prize money and see how long we could party like Elvis and Priscilla. It took me a few months to seriously think about how to execute on the business plan. Friends and family reminded me how unique and special this opportunity was and how I may regret it later if I didn't at least give it a chance. I still had to finish two more semesters in my MBA program. After graduating from the University of Colorado Denver with my MBA in December of 2004, I went all in to start my first business venture in January, just 3 months before my daughter was due. I sat down with my wife, and we went over all the risks and tried our best to come up with back-up plans in case things didn't work out. Ultimately, if we failed, we knew I could still find a job and bounce back within 3-5 years. I also realized that there never really is a good or right time to start a business.

In school, I learned about the various funding channels available to entrepreneurs. However, I came to find out that the type and size of your business, your race, status, and network were important deciding factors for funding your venture. One of the most well-known funding sources for startup entrepreneurs is the Small Business Administration (SBA). I set up meetings with all the major banks in the Denver metro area and the SBA officers that they worked with. Every single SBA officer asked me the same two questions: "Are you a hair stylist or a fashion designer?" and "What personal assets do you have as collateral for the SBA loan?"

When I told them that I did not have any experience in the grooming or retail clothing sectors and I did not own any properties for collateral, they said I was not qualified and denied my application. It certainly was a catch-22. I needed to already own assets valued at the same amount of funding I needed to start my business. Plus, business acumen and branding expertise, albeit outside of my new intended sector, meant nothing. Although I didn't agree, I understood their perspective and logic. I wished I had been better prepared in my MBA education for this first wave of rejections.

I had asked one SBA officer if there were any SBA programs specifically for minorities. This was the first time I used my minority card in my life. The SBA officer said the only ones he knew about were for female-owned businesses. "You are the wrong type of minority anyway," he said.

I asked him to clarify. "Well, you are an Asian, aren't you?" He explained. "You people are smart and well connected within your communities. You don't need any help from the SBA."

I left that meeting completely torn on whether the SBA officer's statement was a compliment or not. I wasn't able to get a loan, so it sucked regardless.

The traditional funding channels were simply not available for me. I had to find creative ways to raise funding if I was seriously going to start this business. The first investment check came from an unexpected but familiar source. Bryan Van Dyke, my supervisor and mentor at Rare Medium. He and I stayed in touch throughout my MBA program. Bryan had introduced me to the leadership at the agency he worked for in Chicago and I completed the first round of interviews before I won the business plan competition. I went to Chicago for the final round of interviews. I stayed the night at Bryan's house, and we went out for beers after the interviews. Before we finished our first pint, Bryan asked, "You're not going to take the offer from our agency, are you?"

I told Bryan about trying to launch MetroBoom, how I might regret it if I didn't try it, and how sorry I was about having to turn down the opportunity to work with him again. To my surprise, he smiled and said, "I would be more disappointed if you took the job. You should take advantage of this opportunity and go about launching your own business."

I thanked him for understanding, and then he surprised me again by offering to be my first investor. I could not believe how blessed I was to have someone like Bryan in my life. I would be surprised and reminded again and again of the many great friends I have been blessed with over the coming months and years.

My startup funding consisted of Bryan's investment, the cash prize from the business plan competition (minus Uncle Sam's cut), student loan consolidation loan, and 10 credit cards. I paid for everything on credit cards to save my cash for operations once we opened. It was amazing what you could pay for with credit cards, even back in 2005. As a bootstrapped entrepreneur, I could not afford to hire contractors for renovations. I had to figure out how I could do everything on my own. I built as many fixtures and pieces of furniture as I could from scratch, and I looked for bargains for everything else I couldn't build. Once again, I was blessed with great friends during this hectic period. Bob Bauman and Devin Porter, two friends I met through the MBA program, came to my rescue. One of Bob's undergraduate degrees was in electrical engineering and he was one of those smart guys who knew a lot about a lot of things. Bob taught me the basics of electricity. He helped me buy the right tools and taught me how to wire and rewire the space per my needs. Devin was an artist at heart and helped me with painting, sanding, and putting the finishing touches on the fixtures I had built. Dennis Graser, a former colleague of mine, also helped me on weekends. My sister Yeon, who graduated from Parsons, lent her interior design expertise to draw up the renovation plans, and helped me implement them. It was a difficult challenge because the space was just over 1,000 square feet and we had to find a way to maximize every square inch. As most siblings are, Yeon and I are opposite in so many ways. However, when it comes to creativity and execution, we complement each other perfectly. We made great partners as we put in countless hours renovating the space together.

This is also true for one of my best friends, Emerson Bonilla. He has supported me from the very beginning of my entrepreneurial journey. Meeting Emerson was one of few good things that came from working in that toxic private branding firm. Along with me, he was one of four minority employees at the firm, and we hit it off right away. When I was getting rejected by every bank in town, Emerson and his wife Mary invited me over for dinner. I was thankful for the home-cooked meal because food is my love language. As we were finishing up the delicious dinner, Emerson and Mary made me an offer that blew my mind. They felt bad for me as they watched me struggle to find funding, and they were afraid that I would never get the chance to launch my idea.

"It kills us that you are having such difficulty with raising your startup capital," they said. "We don't have any cash to invest in your idea, but we wish we did. However, what we do have is our house. We are not sure how much equity we have in this house as we had bought it just few years ago. But if you can use our house as a collateral to raise the money you need, we would be happy to co-sign for you. We believe in you, and we want to help in any way we can."

I wasn't sure what I had done to deserve such kind support and trust from Emerson and Mary. Family members would not even offer their houses as collateral, especially for a rookie entrepreneur. Their words of encouragement and love filled my heart. I respectfully declined their incredibly generous offer and became more determined than ever to launch my business. Emerson continued to support me in so many other ways. He and I drove his brand-new truck overnight to Phoenix to pick up some cool yet affordable furniture from IKEA. In 2005, that was the closest IKEA to Denver. Many people I knew would have been concerned about putting thousands of miles on their brand-new vehicle, but Emerson offered so that I didn't have to rent a truck and save money. Mary even packed us a cooler full of food, snacks, and beverages. We drove through the night and arrived at the IKEA in Phoenix just before they opened on Saturday morning. We went through the aisles like well-trained soldiers, loaded up multiple carts, and checked out in less than two hours. We grabbed lunch and drove straight back to Colorado. Thanks to Emerson, what would have been a dreadfully exhausting trip turned into a fun road trip with a great friend.

Emerson and I built grooming station fixtures in his garage. When I wasn't there, Emerson would pick up where I had left off and worked on the fixtures after he got off work. Emerson also helped me with the dirty demolition work in the space. He even hauled out the trash, debris, and old fixtures to the dumpster. Emerson saved me thousands of dollars and hours of work. His support didn't stop after I opened my business, either. Whenever I needed repairs, upgrades, or remodeling, Emerson was right there. He drove over 30 miles every month to get a haircut at MetroBoom, promoted my business to everyone he knew, and never missed one of our events. Along with Bryan, Emerson was a brother from another mother. I am truly blessed.

The renovations took longer and costed more than I estimated, despite all the help from my friends and sister. We finally launched in October of 2005, two months behind schedule. Based on my primary research, conservative financial assumptions, and average case projections, I expected to hire three stylists and serve 300 clients in the first month. My research had shown that a stylist with 3-5 years of experience typically served 200-300 clients on a monthly basis. What I did not know was that there was an imbalance of supply and demand in the cosmetology industry's labor market. I later learned that an average 30-40% of licensed cosmetology school graduates permanently leave the field after 2-3 years of working. Many of them realize the work is backbreaking and the schedule is rigid. The level of creativity and flexibility they wanted only came after years of building hard-earned experience, a loyal clientele, and an impeccable reputation. The rate of new salons and barbershops opening did not match the number of graduating cosmetologists. In fact, the number of new salons and barbershops steadily increased over time, throwing off the balance between supply and demand. The difficulty of hiring qualified stylists wasn't just a problem for me but was a major problem in the entire industry. I had no idea until I tried hiring my own employees. I somehow managed to hire two stylists before we opened. They both had taken maternity leave and were looking for new opportunities. I got lucky, but it also meant that neither stylists had any current clients of their own to bring to MetroBoom. So instead of what I had researched and expected, we launched with zero clients. I hadn't planned for this to be my worst-case scenario, but it was my reality.

My reserved operating cash and the small number of investments from friends helped me get through the first couple of months as all of my projections went out the window. Inevitably, I ran out of cash few months after opening and had to face the possibility of closing. The cash relief I desperately needed came from multiple sources. An investor who had promised a second round of investment agreed to invest early based on my dire need.

After graduating from the University of Colorado Denver with my MBA, I was invited to return as a guest speaker for the business planning class. I was also invited to various events at the Business School and entrepreneurship center. During one of these events, I got to meet Professor Madhavan Parthasarathy (also known as MP). He taught marketing at CU Denver's Business School. Though I had missed the opportunity to take one of his classes while I was in the program, we immediately hit it off as we shared drinks and our immigrant journeys. Unlike other professors, MP struck me as down to earth, genuine, humble, and funny. He invited me to speak in his classes, came into MetroBoom with his son for haircuts, and met with me for lunch and coffee on a regular basis. I greatly enjoyed our conversations. MP's insightful and supportive advice on life came across as an older brother's perspective, which I greatly appreciated. During one of our regular lunch sessions, I started venting about all my financial and startup struggles with MP. I had become so comfortable with him that I wasn't aware of how long I had been whining. MP stopped me with a simple question and statement. "I don't understand why you are complaining," he said. "Only those who think quitting is an option complain. You are not a quitter, are you? I just don't see you as a quitter."

It felt like a mic drop. I needed to hear that. At our next lunch, MP slid over a check and said he wanted to help. After thanking him for his trust and support, I asked him if he would like to set up the arrangement as a loan or investment. He said he didn't care. MP told me to treat his check however it would serve me best. I told him it would be best to have him as an investor, so I said I would send over an investor agreement. He said not to bother. "No amount of paperwork would stop a dishonest person from cheating someone," he said. "I know you are a person of integrity based on our relationship, your family upbringing, and culture. I trust you."

It was another eye-opening moment for me. In the years to follow, MP would be there for me every step of the way to provide support, guidance, mentorship, opportunities, and motivation. He was also the person who gave me my first opportunity to teach at the University of Colorado Denver. Without his trust and support, I would not have discovered my passion for teaching.

The next funding came on a random Sunday. In those days, I opened on Sundays by myself to sell our clothing and other retail items. Most Sundays, I caught up on bookkeeping and planned out various marketing strategies. On this particular Sunday, my friend Karen called and said she would like to come by. Karen Hertz is one of those few souls who does not have a single malicious atom in her being. She can brighten up any room she walks into without saying a word. She beams positive and happy energy. We sat in my tiny box of an office and, in a concerned "mama bear" tone, she asked how I was doing. I told her the truth about my financial struggles and shared some of the strategies I was trying. Karen expressed how much she believed in me and cared for me as a good friend. Then she took out her checkbook, wrote me a check, and handed it to me. I was caught off guard and asked why she was giving me the check. She told me how tough it was for her to watch me struggle and wanted to help. I was stunned. I knew we were good friends, but I had no idea how much Karen cared about me as a friend. Although she didn't ask for anything in return for her generosity, I insisted on recognizing her contribution as an investment and offering her equity. Karen said she didn't care, but that was the least I could do to respect her money and value our friendship. I had every intention to quadruple her investment and make her proud. Karen's check was the single largest investment I had received. I was beyond grateful as it allowed me to keep MetroBoom open and give it my all. I worked seven days a week, even when the shop was technically closed. I have always worked a minimum of nine to ten hours a day, often many more, but for the first time, I never stopped working. Even when I was home, my brain was running through strategies, tactics, and numbers. The pressure and stress were constant. There was no such thing as getting off work. It was always on. I was always on. There were many mornings when Alexis would be getting up to go to work as I was coming home from work. This was before cloud computing, affordable laptops, and remote working. Whatever work I needed to complete was on my desktop computer at the shop. I also attended every networking opportunity possible, which often included two or three events every day, four or five days a week. My time as a startup founder was free. I needed to hustle at the highest level. No one was more qualified, passionate, and hungry than I was. I averaged 3-4 hours of sleep a night. Some of those hours were on the couch so I wouldn't wake up Alexis. Sleep, food, and water were mere inconveniences as I strived to make my first venture a success. I often told people that I would sleep when I am dead. I believed in this mantra, only to find out how dangerously obtuse it was years later.

Just as MetroBoom hit its stride and was steadily growing, the recession came knocking in 2007. The signs were already there in late 2006. As the economy declined, I faced unanticipated developments and changes in consumer behavior. On the grooming side of our business, we saw our clients going longer in between haircuts, growing their hair out, switching to cheaper franchise salons and barbershops, and shaving their heads with a $10 clipper from Walmart. When I wrote my business plan back in 2004, I could not have imagined ever having to compete against at-home clippers or the Flowbee (Google it for s good laugh if you've never heard of it). On the retail side, it was even worse. My business model leveraged returning grooming clients to purchase our retail clothing and accessories. Male clothing purchases were based on two identifiable cycles in the early 2000s. The first one was to replace an item that had been stained, ripped, or deemed hazardous by a significant other. The second was for special occasions like weddings, interviews, formal work functions, etc. We depended on the traffic from our grooming services to feed our retail sales. When that traffic slowed and our inventory costs outweighed our retail sales revenue, I had to pivot. Oddly enough, my next strategy came from a short friend's struggle with retail clothing.

I grew up with this friend in Korea and had just reconnected with him after 25 years. He was working for a Korean airline at the time and regularly traveled to Colorado. He liked to get his hair cut during these visits so he could see MetroBoom and support me. He also made an honest effort to buy our clothing, but nothing would fit him. One evening, as we sat down for dinner, he shared his struggles with finding clothes that fit him. For formal attire, he had to get custom-tailored clothing in Korea. He said the cost was reasonable and the quality was excellent. He would get measured for shirts, slacks, and jackets in Korea on his business trips and simply pick them up on the next trip back. He promised to wear his custom-tailored clothes on his next trip to Colorado so I could take a close look. Up to this point, our retail items consisted of casual attire, including T-shirts, button-down shirts, jeans, track jackets, and the like. I chose not to carry formal attire because the costs were too high and it was difficult to find the proper fit for customers. I also didn't have a whole lot of knowledge in formal wear. Instead, I had been outsourcing formal wear requests to a local haberdasher who worked with his own custom tailors. I received a 15% referral commission on every custom item my clients would purchase from him. This was the best option for a small startup like mine at the time, as the referral commission did not accrue any costs, only revenue. The haberdasher offered super high-quality items at a much higher price point than MetroBoom's casual offerings. When my friend returned with his custom-tailored clothes from Korea, I was ecstatic. The fabric and stitching quality were superior to most department store brands. The fit was indisputable. Many of our clients were active and had athletic builds, which meant that while shirts and jackets fit their broad shoulders, they were swimming in the midsection. In the mid-2000s, the majority of men's fashion in the U.S. was ill-fitted and boxy for athletic bodies. I was convinced. Custom-tailored clothing would become a critical pivot and a meaningful competitive differentiation for my business. I just had to figure out the financial modeling of this new service and product line, as well as the international manufacturing and supply chain logistics. Oh, and learn how to measure, fit, and consult clients on custom-tailored clothing, which I have never done before.

I immediately called my cousin in Korea. He was a seasoned sales professional and savvy networker. If anyone could help me figure out the custom-tailoring business, it would be him. Within weeks, he found the most ideal Korean tailoring operation for me. My cousin spoke with the owner and persuaded him to meet with me. By this time, the recession was in full effect and I was low on operating cash again. So, I charged my plane ticket to Korea on my credit card and took a big gamble. Alexis thought I was nuts and told me so multiple times. When I arrived in Korea, I met with the owner of the tailoring operation right away. I explained the market in Colorado; its lack of affordable options, absence of serous competitors, and my vision of making custom clothing a consultative and personalized service offering rather than just a merchandise offering. He expressed his skepticism and concern over entering an unproven market with such a disruptive concept. I told him I was willing to do whatever it would take if he would take me on as a client. I think my desperate enthusiasm came through. He reluctantly agreed and trained me on all aspects of his operation, from measuring to stitching on buttons. We agreed to an ordering process, pricing structure, shipping requirements, and payment processing system. This was way before today's online transaction platforms and Google Drive that we have now; all of it was analog. They handed me hard copies of the order sheets where 90% of the required information needed to be handwritten and faxed over. I had to wire money to my cousin's bank account in Korea and have him pay the tailoring company. I had them take my measurements and make 10 shirts so that I could wear and display them for marketing purposes. With 10 custom shirts and two fabric swatch books, I flew back to Colorado with more enthusiasm than desperation.

At the shop, I always had nine shirts on display and wore the tenth one. I would rotate them so there was always a custom shirt on my back and nine others on display right by the entrance and window. The first year, we had about

200 shirt orders. It was a slow start but a promising one. Most of the sales came from grooming clients who saw the marketing collateral, heard my staff and I talk about the custom shirts, saw me wearing one, and/or saw the display. When I sat down with potential clients for consultations and measurements, I intentionally spoke a little louder than normal so that other clients getting haircuts could hear me. This surprisingly worked well. Clients would finish their haircuts and come over to start their own consultations or schedule one for another day as they checked out at the front desk. Having a small space provided an unexpected advantage in this internal marketing tactic. Logistically, it was difficult to measure the clients accurately, fill out the analog order sheets, fax them over to Korea, and confirm shipping schedules. I decided to hire an agent in Korea and work the cost into the pricing. However, our price was still 40-50% lower than the competition. I created an order sheet in Excel with all the technical details and options pre-built into the template. This cut the time to place an order by 75% and reduced the amount of errors on my end by 90%. This also allowed me to email the orders to my agent, which he would then print and fax over to the tailor. The owner of the tailoring company was not happy about these changes. After a few months, he fired me as a client. My cousin and agent found me another tailoring company in Korea to work with whose owner agreed to use the new order sheets I had created. The tailoring process was the same as the first company, so the quality of the clothing did not change. The new custom shirt offering was paying dividends on multiple fronts. I would charge clients the full amount when I placed their orders, but I did not have to pay the tailoring company and my agent until the shipment arrived at my shop. The process of tailoring, quality assurance, international shipping, customs processing, and domestic shipping took roughly 30 days. At this time, the same process for my competitors took 60-90 days and they charged up to 150% more for their custom-tailored clothing. I was able to provide quality products through a highly personalized service that was faster and more affordable than others. This was a critical competitive advantage that my brand could own. Operationally, the prepayment from the clients gave me the cash

flow for 30 days until I paid my vendor in Korea. This demand-generated sales model that I had learned from Dell back at Gray Advertising in the mid 90's immensely increased the viable sustainability of my business. I had often heard from seasoned entrepreneurs that "cash flow is king." Indeed, it was.

While the custom shirts were just taking off, I still had serious cash flow issues. The additional revenue seemed promising, but it grew at a pace that wasn't providing any immediate relief to my operational cash shortfall. Banks weren't willing to lend to a small, novel business concept like mine, especially when I didn't have any personal collateral. I was also behind on paying the federal employment tax. I had made a point to pay on a quarterly basis to avoid a huge lump sum at the end of the year, per my CPA's advice. However, during the recession, I faced a tough choice between paying the IRS or rent. I called a fellow entrepreneur and friend for advice. I expressed my grave predicament of having no access to loans and falling behind on the federal employment tax. He definitely had a more aggressive entrepreneurial approach than I did. He gave me some solid advice and I decided to follow some of it. He told me to swipe my own personal credit cards that had 0% APR which I had been saving for a rainy day on the credit card machine at MetroBoom. The transaction would dump cash into my business checking account the next day. It was a normal transaction and not a cash advance, therefore the 0% APR would still apply for the next 12 months. I was able to cover payroll and rent by cannibalizing my personal credit cards to create operational cash for my business. However, I didn't have enough to pay the federal employment tax. My buddy told me not to pay the employment tax until the IRS called me on a weekly basis for the delinquency in payment. He said they would start with periodic payment reminder letters. The periodic letters would become monthly, paired with periodic calls. Then the calls would become monthly, and eventually weekly along with more threatening letters. I was only able to take half of his advice on this one because my risk tolerance was not as high as his. I waited until the letters became monthly, which was about a year in, during which time the custom-tailored shirts were generating enough revenue to significantly improve our cash flow. I eventually called the IRS to set up a payment program for the owed federal employment tax. The monthly payment plan was around $250, including penalties and interest payments. Although it was scary as hell to make the IRS wait for overdue taxes, I think it was the right decision for me at the time. I was able to wait it out by choosing to pay rent and improve our cash flow. The eviction process would have been a lot quicker than a year.

Using credit cards for startup costs and leveraging personal credit cards to cover payroll during the recession were high-risk decisions that I wouldn't recommend to anyone. However, I did what I had to do to launch and maintain my business. I also did the best I could to manage the risk with discipline. I frequently transferred balances from one credit card to another to take advantage of 0% APR promotions and lock in lower APRs for the lifetime of the balance. Even with balance transfer fees, the savings from the 0% promotional APRs and lower APRs were always higher. I was able to pay off the principle balance much quicker. By 2012, seven years into our operation, I had paid off 90% of our debt. The frequent and disciplined balance transfers kept the overall cost of used capital just under 6%, which is remarkable considering that prime rates were as high as 8.25% during this period.

The word was spreading, and my custom-tailored shirt business was growing. With growth came additional needs and demands though. Clients asked about ways to personalize their shirts with design options, accents, and creative fabrics. I went out to Korea again to meet with the tailoring company and see about their willingness and capabilities to take on more personalization options. Once again, the vendor fired me as a client. They refused to deviate from their operational procedures to accommodate my clients' wants. I understood their position. I didn't have enough volume to justify these changes on their end. I was just a small fish in their pool of large-volume clients. My agent also expressed concerns over finding a tailoring company that would meet my clients' wants. He introduced me to another agent as he also fired me as a client. Things could not have gone any worse. Like they say, when one door closes, another opens. Sometimes the new door is bigger and leads to better things. The new agent turned out to be much more of a business partner who I could rely on. Our values aligned much more closely, and she treated my business as her own. She also found a tailoring company whose owner was more entrepreneurial and creative. I was able to negotiate with the new tailoring company to take on the personal design options that my clients wanted. The unit cost per shirt would increase, but the tailoring company would not charge for the design options à la carte. This was a critical juncture in my custom shirt business. Locking in a per unit cost allowed me to provide a fully customized experience, and the clients were willing to pay for the extra design services. The additional design options started as low as $5 per option and my clients could add as many or as few as they wanted. By the time my clients completed their design specs, each shirt would average around $150 compared to the $100 base price. The ability for customization proved to be a powerful motivation for my clients to return for more shirts and recommend us to others. When they were wearing their custom-designed shirts in public, MetroBoom clients stood out. Wives and girlfriends would set up consultation sessions with me to design shirts for surprise gifts. Our order volume grew and so did our margins thanks to the à la carte design options. I was able to pivot our tailored clothing business model from outsourcing to a haberdasher at a meager 15% referral commission in the beginning to a healthy margin of 100-125% under our own private label. Subsequently, we expanded our offerings to include suits, sports coats, slacks, coats, and ties. Our design options for custom shirts also expanded to over 30 variations. We went through a few more tailoring vendors, but my agent stuck with me every step of the way. We also found that the custom design options were not easy for competitors to copy as it required changing operational procedures and slowed down the pace. We were able to carve out a niche in the market and enjoy this monopoly for a while. Expanding our custom-tailored clothing offerings through the manufacturing supply chain in Korea directly contributed to reaching profitability in the fifth year of our operation.

As MetroBoom grew, so did the confidence for my vision. I did not launch MetroBoom so I could have a mom-and-pop business. My vision was to create a consumer retail brand from scratch and build it to a national level. Scaling the business was always on my mind. Reaching profitability and distributing dividends to my investors were catalytic milestones leading up to that goal. I began the process of inviting hand-picked, loyal clients to small focus groups. I facilitated multiple sessions to solicit their feedback on what new services and products they would like to see from us. I asked what services, amenities, and products they are purchasing elsewhere that we could offer. I would then finish the sessions by asking what services, amenities, and products they would like but couldn't find anywhere. Their feedback was invaluable. Not only was I able to gather insightful market and customer data, but I also engaged my clients on a deeper level with MetroBoom's brand. I conducted thorough research and analysis on their feedback, the competitive market, feasibility of their suggestions, and financial modeling.

After months of grueling but exciting work, I was able to create the strategy for MetroBoom 2.0. It consisted of moving into a larger space to house new and enhanced services, amenities, and products. I began searching for the new space with a client who was a commercial real estate broker. After months of searching, we found an ideal property. The building was originally constructed to be a small mansion on the east side of downtown Denver. A retail space was added to the front of the mansion years later. Its old-school architectural charm and modern renovations created the perfect combination for MetroBoom 2.0. The financials also worked out. I would be able to complete most of the renovations myself and keep the budget under $30,000. Plus, the increase in rent would be manageable. I signed the lease and gave notice to vacate the current space. I began working with an architect, who was also a MetroBoom client to draw up the renovation plans for our tenant improvement permit while I began working on projects that didn't require the permit: new building fixtures, painting, and cleaning. When I went to file for the tenant improvement permit, I didn't know this seemingly simple process would kick off the long and painful journey that would lead to my demise. I was notified by the building department that the property was deemed unsound because the building owner failed to keep it up to code with the required upgrades and maintenance. I was also told that until the building owner brings the entire property back up to code, there was nothing I could do as the tenant. I would not be able to renovate or operate my business out of the building. I immediately called the building owner. She accused the building department of "not liking her personally and coming after her building unjustly." She played dumb when I asked about the building code violations and the unsafe structural state of the building. I needed immediate action from her, but she had no intentions of doing right by the building department or my business. MetroBoom's current space was already rented out to a new tenant because the area had become very popular. It was too late to ask to stay in the space, and we didn't have the time to secure another building. I was left without a physical location to operate my brick-and-mortar business. On the last Friday and Saturday of May 2013, about half a dozen of my most loyal clients came to help me pack up my entire business in boxes and move them into my garage at home. They voluntarily spent their free time to help me. It meant the world to have these gentlemen by my side on the darkest day of my entrepreneurial journey. I didn't have the luxury to sulk in self-pity as I had to continue operating my business in the absence of a physical space. For the grooming side of my business, I rented a couple of chairs at a client's nearby beauty salon. My trusted mentor and friend, MP, offered the incubation space at the Jake Jabs Center for Entrepreneurship for me to conduct our custom clothing consultations. MP's commitment and unyielding support for hustling entrepreneurs saved my business. Although some clients expressed their discomfort with walking into a university building for their custom clothing needs, our loyal clients stuck with us. While I was grateful for the two temporary locations to continue my business, it was far from an ideal operation. In fact, it was physically exhausting and emotionally demoralizing. I just had to grit through this temporary hardship until I found a new home for my business. As weeks turned into months, my self-doubt and desperation grew rampant. During this detrimental chapter of my professional life, I was blindsided by a fatal blow in my personal life.

I felt under the weather on a particular Sunday as I joined my son for his afternoon nap. My wife had taken my daughter to run errands. My phone was in the living room, and I had passed out next to my son. At the sound of my name, I jolted awake and heard my wife yelling from the front door. She screamed that my father was sick and my mom had been desperately trying to call me. My mom eventually called my wife after she kept getting my voicemail. I called my mother back in a daze, got dressed, and drove over to my parents' place. I still regret not particularly speeding through the 45-minute drive, but I had no idea of the magnitude of my father's situation.

By the time I arrived at their house, an ambulance had taken my father to the nearest hospital and my mother was calmly preparing to head over there with me. I misread her quiet demeanor as a sign that my father's condition wasn't serious. I should have remembered my mom's innate ability to remain calm even in the most terrifying of situations, just like the time she witnessed my father getting robbed at gunpoint. We arrived at the hospital and stood in the emergency room's waiting area. I was still clueless when the ER doctor came over to explain my father's condition. Suddenly, his pager went off to signal the rapid decline in my father condition, and we were led to the critical care unit. Finally, it all clicked in my thick head. A long line of nurses trailed outside of Room 13 where my father was placed. They were taking turns to perform CPR. Minutes passed as the nurses rotated through at a frantic pace. Finally, the ER doctor dismissed them and said that my father was in a stable condition.

We were led in to see him. He was unconscious, his skin had an unfamiliar gray hue, and he had multiple tubes going in and out of his body. I stood there in bewilderment, unable to keep my thoughts straight or still. My mom bent down to hold his hand and tried to talk him into waking up. A few seconds later, the machines my father was hooked up to started going off with piercing alarms and flashing lights. My father's body started to jerk frantically. My mother screamed for my father to wake up and begged him not to leave us. She looked up at me with a level of desperation I had never seen in her eyes before and asked me to join her in begging my father not to leave. I could not squeeze out a single word, not even a murmur. I froze. Nurses rushed in, and they asked us to step outside. We stood in the hallway and watched the nurses form a line again to revive my father. My mother stood with her eyes closed and prayed with her hands clasped in front of her. I watched a full rotation of nurses cycle through when the ER doctor approached me. She told me that my father's heart had spiraled into a deathly rhythm and was only beating because of the CPR effort from the nurses. The doctor asked me if I would give the permission to stop the CPR. I thought I had misunderstood her question in my dazed state of mind, so I asked her to clarify.

"Are you asking me to kill my father?" I asked.

She explained the irreversible condition my father had fallen into and the hospital's policy to require a family member's permission in order to stop the CPR. Her heartfelt advice was to let my father go. My mom broke away from her prayer to ask me what the doctor was saying. I translated the doctor's initial request and my mom repeatedly screamed a stern no. I translated more of the doctor's explanation about my father's inevitable outcome. I cannot remember how long I stood there looking at my mom or if my mom ever gave me a verbal or nonverbal response. But I turned to the doctor and nodded to end my father's life. Many family members and close friends have tried to console me on what I did that night. They said I didn't have a choice. They said I didn't technically end my father's life. They said it was a required medical decision that was ultimately best for my father. While I appreciated everyone's empathy and love in their efforts to alleviate my burden, I see it differently. The fact is my father's last heartbeat was determined by my decision. My nod brought the end to his life, medically required or not. That is a fact I have to live with for the rest of my life. That is a burden that will always be present in my consciousness. Maybe the weight of my remorse would not be as heavy if I had treated my father better when he was alive. I had opportunities, an abundance of them, to change my judgmental perspective of my father and improve our relationship, but I passed on them every time. It is now the biggest regret of my life. It also serves as a powerful reminder for me to make sure I do not let another opportunity slip away from me, regardless of how big or small.

During this time, my inner voice of doubt and fear cranked its volume dial to 11. In my desperate attempt to prove to myself and everyone else that I could overcome this challenge, I started to make unsound financial decisions to reopen my business in a new space. I signed a lease for an unfinished space in an up-and-coming neighborhood that was off the beaten path. This meant that I had to pay the high costs of finishing the space with basic necessities and utilities like drywall, plumbing, electricity, HVAC, etc. The cost of building out an empty shell into a functional space and obtaining a certificate of occupancy was a lot higher than what my small business could afford. In my tunnel vision to reopen and not allow the dishonest building owner to ruin my business, I made a series of decisions that destroyed my budget. I signed for every loan, line of credit, and credit card deal to access as much capital as the new buildout required.

One Friday afternoon, a loyal client and friend sat down with me for coffee. Joe Fuyuno had just moved to Denver from New York City when he came into MetroBoom the first time. We immediately hit it off. Over the next few years, he became an integral member of the 20% of clients who generated 80% of our revenue. Joe also shared some cool ideas from around the world (he was an avid traveler and had exquisite taste) and referred us to every person he came across. He was also one of the loyal clients who helped us move my business into my garage back in May. Joe expressed his genuine concern for where my business was heading. He suggested that I call it quits and go back to consulting. Joe was able to see what I could not at the time. He assured me that I had a good run and it was time to let go. Joe was being a true friend. However, I disagreed with his suggestion. I told Joe that I could not let down all the clients who had been patiently waiting for us to reopen in our new space. He was forced to simply sit by and watch me run towards my demise. He supported me and MetroBoom to the bitter end. For his loyal friendship and support, I am forever grateful.

It was 419 days after I packed up and moved my business into my garage when I finally reopened in the new space. The launch of MetroBoom 2.0 was two years behind schedule. I stayed true to the vision my clients had helped me build from those focus groups. I maintained the grooming and custom clothing services while introducing new amenities and services: a bar, event space, shared working space, meeting rooms, membership programs, and private liquor lockers. These were all the things my clients had told me they wanted back in 2013. Unfortunately, during the 419 days, many of our clients found other businesses to meet their needs. Some of the new ideas I wanted to launch had already been launched by others. As disappointing as it was, I could not blame those clients for leaving us. The delay had been just too long, and the costs of doing business with us rose above their toleration. I realized I was the poor sucker who threw a party only to have no one show up in those cheesy movies from the 80s. It felt terrible, but I didn't have time to dwell on it; I had payroll, rent, and loan payments to worry about. I had to make major changes in my business strategy and operational model to make it work. I took on my largest consulting engagement to date and was determined to do whatever it takes to keep MetroBoom going. I worked around the clock doing consulting, MetroBoom operations, custom clothing consultations, hosting events, speaking, teaching, etc. I desperately needed the income from consulting, speaking, and teaching to keep MetroBoom afloat. My business was no longer profitable. I didn't have time to sleep. I barely remembered to eat and drink during my hectic daily grind. I poured 8-10 cups of coffee into my body every day followed by quadruple shots of espresso in the evening before teaching. This ridiculous amount of caffeine successfully tricked my brain and body to keep going. I was determined more than ever to keep it going, grit it out, and never give up.

My mom's 70th birthday came and went without a proper celebration per her request. After my father's passing, she didn't feel it was appropriate. In 2016, as a belated birthday celebration, I planned our first mom-and-son trip. One of my best friends, Jason Regier, was playing in a tournament in Vancouver, Canada. Jason is an accomplished wheelchair rugby player who has won multiple Paralympic medals and world championships. Along with his U.S. national team members, Jason was competing in Vancouver to qualify for the upcoming Paralympic Games in Brazil. Jason and I met during our last semester in the MBA program at the University of Colorado Denver. Despite our different backgrounds and upbringing, we quickly became close friends. Jason and I collaborated on many projects together. He was instrumental in helping me land the large consulting engagement I was working on. Jason is also the reason why I began my professional speaker career. While the guest speaking seemed enough for me at the time, Jason instilled the confidence in me to acknowledge my talent and passion for public speaking. As a regular guest speaker, Jason has been inspiring my students by sharing his triumphant journey from his life-altering injury to accomplishing the highest accolade in athletic competitions all over the world. In the 15 years of our friendship, Jason has been the constant source of inspiration for me to push forward and confidant to ground me so I could focus on the important things in life. Just like my mom, Jason is always cool under pressure and balances out my innate East-coast impatience. People often stare at us with a puzzled expression when we hang out in public. Nothing you see on the surface would readily explain how we can be such close friends.

We are definitely an odd couple demographically, geographically, culturally, and racially. However, we share something a lot deeper and fundamental, our personal brand values. I am grateful for Jason's presence and impact in my life.

My mom had never seen the thrilling game of wheelchair rugby in person before, so I thought it would be a win-win to visit the city and attend the tournament. The plan was to fly into Seattle, rent a car, and drive up to Vancouver. After the tournament, we would drive back to Seattle and visit the same family friends who helped us moved from New York to Colorado way back in 1993.

My mom was really excited about the trip. I couldn't remember the last time I had seen her this excited. She was even thrilled about the rental car, as she had never rented a car before. I should have reserved something nicer than a Hyundai. The drive up to Vancouver was as beautiful as people had told me. We checked into our cozy Airbnb in a bustling neighborhood close to the downtown area. The one-bedroom unit had a great view of the city and mountains behind the skyline. My mom took the bedroom and I slept on a comfortable pull-out couch in the living room. We watched Jason play the last few games of the tournament and met up with an old friend of mine from college who took us around to see the city's tourist hotspots. My mom visited the local farmers' market a few blocks away from our Airbnb and picked up local produce and fresh catches of the day. My mom, who is a wonderful chef, made fantastic dishes with the fresh ingredients, and we ate together at the tiny two-person dining table. We ate, drank, talked, and laughed as if we were a couple of life-long friends kicking back together. I still remember how we savored our last meal. My mom made ramen with fresh seafood from the farmer's market. It was a simple dish, but it had a depth of flavor I had not tasted in ramen before. The few days we spent in Vancouver was everything I had hoped for on our first mom and son trip.

Afterward, we drove back down to Seattle to stay with the same family friends who left New York City with us 23 years ago. They welcomed us with open arms and consoled us on my father's passing. We reminisced about the old days back in New York. My mom and I drove around Seattle to sightsee and had a touristy lunch at Pike Place Market. We then drove back to our family friends' house in the afternoon. I decided to take a quick nap as I was unusually tired. I had dinner plans later that evening with a client, and friend, who had moved back to Seattle a couple of years prior. I was excited to see Doug, his wife Hailey, and their baby daughter Harper. After a quick nap, I drove down to a quaint, lakeside restaurant to meet Doug and his family. The dinner conversation was sweet and spicy, just like my fish tacos. It was just a couple of old friends sharing stories of the good old days while not missing any opportunity for affectionate chop-busting. Doug and I could always give each other a hard time with humor without ever offending each other. I thoroughly enjoyed his clever and quick wit. We wrapped up the conversation before it got too late as I also had plans to go visit another friend before the end of the night.

During dinner, I had felt spurts of subtle chest pain and dizziness. I contributed both to the spicy tacos and dehydration. I only had one beer, so it could not have been the alcohol. I also had never experienced anything like this, so it was natural for me to dismiss it without much thought. As we all got up from the table, I felt like everything was spinning around me. I think I closed my eyes for a moment because, when things came into focus again, Doug and his wife were laughing. I thought I had missed a joke.

"I think I blacked out for a second," I said before everything went black again. When I came to for the second time, I was staring up at the cloudy evening sky. Everything was still blurry. I didn't know what was happening.

"You are in Seattle, and I am your friend Doug," Doug was yelling into my ear, kneeling next to me. "I am here with Hailey and Harper."

"What the hell are you doing, Doug? I know who you are. Why are you telling me all this?"

I thought I said this out loud, but then I realized I was just thinking it. I could not move my mouth. In fact, I couldn't move anything. All I could do was blink. As seconds passed, I heard another voice. A female voice I didn't recognize.

"Jung, squeeze my hand. I am holding your left hand. I want you to squeeze it. Squeeze my hand."

I was confused as to who this was, why she was asking me to squeeze her hand, and why she is holding my hand. By this time, I could hear Doug's voice more clearly.

"You are going to be ok Jung," he said. "Everything is going to be fine."

I was finally able to turn my head to look at Doug. He looked like shit. He was pale as a ghost. I still wasn't able to speak; my mouth felt like it was welded shut. I was able to turn my head to the other side and finally saw the owner of the strange voice asking me to squeeze her hand. I squeezed her hand, and she looked relieved. I turned back to Doug and was finally able to ask, "What happened?"

"You blacked out, buddy," he said. "You just fell over as you told me you thought you had blacked out for a second. Your heart had stopped, and your face turned black so we did CPR on you."

The paramedics arrived. They began checking my vitals when I felt something in my pants. Doug was still kneeling by my head, so I turned to him and whispered, "I think I pooped." I don't know exactly when it happened but there was a fresh load in my pants. The feeling of a full diaper was strange and yet familiar. I did not enjoy it at all. The paramedics wanted to transport me to the ER, but I refused.

"My mom will be worried," I said. I asked Doug to take me to his house so I could get cleaned up before I went back to the family friend's house. Reluctantly, the paramedics left me in Doug's care. Somehow, I had the wherewithal to ask Doug to drive my rental Hyundai so that my poopy pants didn't stink up his car. Doug and Hailey were generous enough to allow me to use their guest bathroom to get cleaned up. Doug lent me a pair of his shorts to wear and drove me back to the family friend's house. When I got there, I did my best to seem nonchalant as I lied to my mom about what happened at the restaurant, but to no avail. My mom first asked, then demanded, the truth. I finally told her that I had blacked out, probably due to dehydration. She was not convinced, but she stopped her interrogation so that I could rest. I laid myself down, but soon realized that my head was burning up while my body was freezing. I felt scared. I called Doug and asked him to take me to the ER. While we were driving to the closest ER, Doug shared more details about what had happened at the restaurant. He said that when I passed out, my head hit the cement pavement of the restaurant patio so hard and loud that he expected a pool of blood to appear around my head. According to Doug, my head fell right next to the feet of a retired nurse having dinner with her husband. She jumped over to take my pulse immediately. She said that I wasn't breathing and that my heart had stopped. She ordered Doug to start mouth-to-mouth resuscitation while she began chest compressions. This retired nurse got my heart beating again before the paramedics arrived. I could have died or had severe brain damage if it hadn't been for her. She was the stranger who asked me to squeeze her hand. In the most urgent moment of my life, my head landed next to the feet of a trained angel who brought me back to life. I am one lucky bastard.

At the ER, they ran a bunch of tests and diagnosed me with a concussion. They could not explain why my heart had stopped and told me to follow up with my primary care physician back home. The burning and freezing sensation disappeared by the time I was released. Doug drove me back to my family friend's house. I did my best to rest that night and the next day as we were scheduled to fly back to Colorado the day after. Against my friends' objections, I drove back to the Seattle airport and returned the rental car. It was one of the most difficult things I have ever done because I was so exhausted, had double vision, and my head was killing me. Looking back, it was a stupid decision, but I didn't want to bother my friends anymore and worry my mom. I felt like I had put them through enough, so I pretended I was fine.

In the weeks and months that followed, I grew more and more frustrated and confused about why this had happened to me. After multiple heart and stress tests, my doctor recommended an electrophysiology (EP) study to see if my heart had an abnormal heartbeat or an arrhythmia issue. The doctor described the procedure as quite evasive. They were going to put me under anesthesia, insert a specialized electrode catheter through my groin to reach my heart, deliver electric shocks to my heart, and record its electrical activity. This was meant to basically recreate what may have happened to me in Seattle, study my heart's reaction, and determine an accurate diagnosis. In layman's terms, they were going to try killing me so they could find out what went wrong with my heart, then figure out how to stop it from happening again. This sounded asinine, but what do I know? I am not a doctor. This scary procedure was unfortunately scheduled on the same day as my son's first day of kindergarten. As I took pictures with Mateo in his kindergarten classroom that morning, my inner voice was screaming that this would be my last day on this earth: Give your boy a goodbye kiss. The next time he will see you will be at your funeral. My fear intensified even more when I signed the waiver form while lying on the hospital bed. I wanted to tell my wife to take good care of our children and wait at least a year before getting remarried to some other schmuck if anything happened to me during the procedure. But I didn't want to be a drama king and show how weak I was to Alexis, so I didn't say anything. I wished for my inner voice to shut the hell up, but I wasn't so lucky.

I woke up four hours later to the Alexis's smiling face. The results from the procedure weren't as welcoming, though. My doctors could not conclusively diagnose anything. They said my heart was fine and the procedure did not reveal why my heart had stopped earlier in the summer. However, they said they inserted an implantable loop recorder in my chest to keep an eye on my heart. When I asked for how long they would keep this device inside my chest, they said three years. I was so frustrated. I wanted an official diagnosis so I could take the right medications, receive the right surgeries, or make the right diet and lifestyle changes to fix it. Instead, I was left with the same confusion as before the evasive procedure. Plus, I gained a mechanical friend inside my chest.

Fittingly, the best diagnosis came from the person who gave me life. My mom shared her diagnosis with true love and brutal honesty in a way that only a mother could. She said I should not be surprised about my body quitting on me after the years of stress I've put it through. After sleeping only 3-4 hours a night, not eating properly, not drinking water, and overriding my brain and body with caffeine for 11 years, it's easy to see why my body shut down. While Alexis, my sister, and close friends expressed similar concerns as my mother's diagnosis before the black-out incident, I had always dismissed them. However, I was finally able to hear them this time. However, I couldn't ignore the realities of my failing business, my commitment to the investors, my pride to succeed, and the injustice of the dishonest building owner's actions. I was not going to quit. I wasn't a quitter. After a few weeks of prescribed rest to recover from the concussion, I went right back to an 80-hour work week. I was determined to make it all work.

Three months after the black-out incident, my life trajectory suddenly changed. On this particular week, Alexis was out of town on a business trip, so I had to take on the sole parenting duties while I ran MetroBoom, did my consulting work, and facilitated three sessions at Denver Startup Week. It was Thursday, and I was driving to work and checking my Facebook feed at red lights and stop signs. I noticed multiple posts about a friend of mine, so I thought it must be his birthday. Later that night, after a long day of work, I picked up my phone to catch up on emails and social media. When I got to checking Facebook, I realized it wasn't my friend's birthday, but he had passed away unexpectedly.

Dan and I met back in 2010. At the time, I was considering moving my custom tailoring operation to a different country due to the rising costs in Korea. I looked into Vietnam, Cambodia, Thailand, Columbia, and Mexico. A friend of mine offered to connect me to Dan, her close friend, a thriving entrepreneur who grew up in California and was living in Bangkok at the time. Dan was married and had two beautiful children. His son was the same age as mine and his daughter was just an infant when we first met. Dan generously agreed to research the custom tailoring industry in Bangkok and line up meetings with a few select operations, just as my cousin did a few years before. So, I flew out to Bangkok to meet Dan and the potential vendors. Dan treated me like a brother from the second we met. It was as if we had known each other for a long time. He made me feel like we were family. He generously spent hours attending meetings with me, translating the discussions, and providing me with his keen entrepreneurial read on each vendor. In between and after meetings, he fed me and took me to his favorite Thai massage centers. He did all this as a favor to our mutual friend. In our conversations, we discovered how similar we were. He was the oldest son in his family and had a younger sister just like I did. In Asian culture, being the oldest son comes with some serious responsibilities, which Dan and I both embraced. He was the same age as me and his son was the same age as mine. He grew up as an Asian man in the U.S. and experienced racism just like I did. He started his entrepreneurial journey without a silver spoon, not even a silver toothpick, just like I did. His personal and entrepreneurial journey was almost identical to mine. We found comfort, mutual respect, and camaraderie with each other. Dan and I encouraged each other to keep pushing, hustling, and grinding as entrepreneurs. We felt a close connection as we shared the same perspective on making personal sacrifices to bring success and happiness to our families. We remained in contact through Facebook and exchanged emails, but we were never able to see each other in person after the first trip to Bangkok.

I followed his funeral proceedings on Facebook in the days after his passing. His family's and friends' posts were heartbreaking and eye opening. Their words, pictures, and videos tore through my heart. It didn't feel like a friend had passed away, which would be tragic as is. It felt like a part of me had passed away. Dan and I had been the same age, striving towards the same goal as entrepreneurs, with aging parents and young children. When I learned more about how Dan passed away, it hit me hard. Dan was driving when he blacked out. He was alone in his car, and he didn't have a retired nurse sitting nearby to save him. If I had blacked out just 10 minutes later in the car as I had planned to go visit another friend, I would have ended up the same as Dan. While I was processing just how incredibly lucky I was, I read about how Dan's family and friends had been concerned about his stress levels, how he didn't sleep enough, how he was working all the time, and how he didn't take care of himself. These concerns penetrated my thick head with both déjà vu and remorse. My own family and friends had been expressing the same concerns about me for years. Like Dan, I proudly wore these behaviors like badges of honor. I was morbidly obtuse in my thinking.

The second wake-up call thundered through my heart when I saw a picture of Dan's son at the funeral. Dan's son was 5 years old at the time, just like my Mateo. He had his tiny hand on Dan's coffin and was looking away with a complex expression. I imagined he was deeply sad and confused about what was happening. I assumed some adults told him that his dad was in the wooden box he was touching and explained what it meant to be dead. I assumed some adults told him that his dad was in heaven and that he would see him again someday. I assumed some adults told him that his dad will always be in his heart. I assumed all this 5-year-old boy wanted was to see his dad again. I naturally thought of my own 5-year-old son. The image of Mateo standing next to my coffin with his own perplexed expression pierced through my heart. I had not learned a single thing from my own experience back in June. I reflected on my mom's honest and blunt diagnosis and how I hadn't changed a single thing in my life since then. In fact, I had become even more stubborn to make things work. I was no longer driven to achieve success; I was driven by the fear of failure. It was like I wasn't in control anymore. I thought long and hard over the next few days. I reflected on my journey as an entrepreneur, professional, student, and teacher. After moving to the U.S., I never took my foot off the gas pedal. I had been in the driver seat with my eyes locked on success. It wasn't until I was screwed over by that dishonest building owner that I found myself in the passenger seat being driven closer and closer toward a "fatal exit." I needed to get back in the driver seat again and regain control. In order to do so, I needed to make the most difficult decision in my life.

I lived with the word on my mind for a month. It took me another month to verbally communicate the word out loud. It took yet another month to carry out the word as an actionable task. The word was to "fail," and it resulted in bankruptcy. The process of thinking, accepting, preparing for, and legally filing to "fail" took me four months. It was the darkest time of my life. Just a few months ago, failure had not been in my vocabulary and bankruptcy had never been an option in my business plan. I had become a statistic of failure, another small business ending in bankruptcy. I felt like I let down my family, friends, investors, staff, and clients. My first stint on my entrepreneurial journey lasted 11 years before coming to an end.

What does Success mean to You?

I have worked in many rooms throughout my teaching and speaking career. Over the last eight years, I have asked the same question to my students, audience members, and clients: What does success mean to you?

I have received hundreds of definitions. Every person should have their own definition of success that is relevant and meaningful to who they are and what they want. Each person's definition of success should absolutely be subjective and personal. There is no right or wrong definition, but there are good and bad ones. After I ask people to come up with their own definition, I follow up with some other probing questions. How did you arrive at that definition? Where did it come from? Why is that so important to you? How do you go about practicing or living out that definition? Some people are left wondering and are unable to come up with authentic answers on the spot. Some shoot back defensive and reactive answers without any truth behind them. Others simply get confused or annoyed. Many people's definition of success consists of borrowed words from popular books, articles, podcasts, and TED talks. Some inherit definitions from their parents and other role models. Extrinsically motivated definition is a bad definition of success.

One of the popular definitions I have heard repeatedly is "financial freedom."

After my usual follow-up questions that I just mentioned, I ask a final question that typically leaves people with a "deer in headlights" expression.

How much do you need to buy your freedom?

Over the past eight years, I've only had two people who actually had developed financial models to estimate how much it would cost to earn their success of "financial freedom." If your definition of success in life is "financial freedom," shouldn't you create your own financial models like those two people and know how much you need to achieve your success? If you do not have a clear and precise definition of success and a way to measure your progress, how would you ever know when you achieved it? How would you know that you are on the right path?

Many definitions of success in life are materialistic and destination-focused goals that are largely short-term oriented. Defining, establishing, prioritizing, and achieving goals can be very effective in life but only on a short- or mid-term basis. When you achieve a goal, the task is completed. Either you set another goal or you come to a full stop. When I talk about success in life, I mean something much more long-term. It is not materialistic in nature or something you can buy and own as property. It's not even a certain amount of cash in the bank. As we all know, material assets can disappear at any given time.

The financial models of those two individuals weren't designed to estimate their ideal amount of money. Instead, money was factored in as the means to provide their financial freedom and pursue their true success in life: traveling, painting, writing, cooking, farming, etc. I loved that they knew what they wanted out of life and had built a model to help them go after it. This intrinsically motivated definition is a good definition of success. According to Dictionary.com, "success" is defined as follows:

Success [*suhk-ses*] [1]

1. The favorable or prosperous termination of attempts or endeavors; the accomplishment of one's goals.

2. The attainment of wealth, position, honors, or the like.

These two are the most popular definitions that most of us use and associate with success. However, there is one more definition we seldom think about:

3. Obsolete.

How would you like it if you worked all your life toward something that is obsolete? You wouldn't. Nobody with a sound mind would.

Search for the word "success" on Google Images. Inevitably, you will see a picture (or several) of a person or people on a mountain top with their arms raised in celebration of their triumph. Reaching the peak of a mountain is a readily accepted and known visual metaphor for success in our society and culture. We also associate other similar metaphors with the pursuit of success: mapping out the fastest route to the top (of companies, industries, subject matters, etc.); climbing with grit, determination, and perseverance while carrying heavy loads of baggage; and more. Let's accept this popular metaphor of success and congratulate these people at the top who have "made it." They worked their butts off climbing to the top and achieving their success. Congratulations! Now what? Are they going to stay up there, on the top of a mountain? Are they expecting to live out a Fairy-tale ending now that they've achieved success? Is that sustainable? Some may say that they will go after another success or climb another mountain. Great! But before you climb another mountain, you must first get down from the one that you are standing on. Did you know the majority of deaths on mountain climbing expeditions happen on the way down?

---

[1] "Success," Dictionary.com, accessed May 10, 2020, https://www.dictionary.com/browse/success

No matter how we slice and dice this destination-driven idea of success, it is flawed. There is no guarantee that you may live long enough to reach that destination. Even if you are lucky enough to reach it, you will be forced to climb down and risk it all again to reach for another. This common and flawed definition of success must be dismantled. Goals can be destination-focused and something that you work hard to accomplish in the short-term. Success, however, is a lifetime pursuit; it evolves, stays fluid, does not come with a checkbox, and does not have a straight road leading to the finish line. It also should not be easy to define. If a term like "financial freedom" immediately comes to your mine, you must question the reason why. Whose voice is that? Is that your term? Is that what you want? Or is that coming from someone or something else? Is that what someone else wants for you? This may come across as a cliché (though I think it is true), but nothing worth having comes easy in life. Doing the right thing is always harder and takes longer. Defining and pursuing your own understanding of success is not supposed to be easy. Even the word "success" demonstrates the difficult nature of the definition itself. Carefully enunciate each part of the word: *suhk-ses*. A big part of success is that it sucks. The process of defining, prioritizing, pursuing, and sacrificing to achieve success sucks. There is nothing easy about it but, ultimately, it is worth it. Nothing else should be more important than defining and owning what is most important in your life.

My clients, students, and audience members consistently and interchangeably use three words when they talk about success: satisfaction, fulfillment, and happiness. Some used these three words to describe what they want out of life. Some said these three words represent success in life. Some used the adverse forms of these three words to describe what they are struggling with in life: dissatisfaction, nonfulfillment, and unhappiness. Regardless of how these three words are used, they are very different from each other. They all do not mean the same thing. As we strive to define what we would like and what is most important to us in life, we must be precise, clear, and focused. Anything less will inevitably lead us down a path of confusion, disappointment, and anxiety. After all, we are talking about what is most important in life. It deserves deep consideration, reflection, and work.

I took a deeper look into these three words for myself. What do they mean to me? Are they important in my life? Which one is more important? Are they independent from each other or interdependent? Do they share a linear or circular relationship? Well, I geeked out. Here is what I came up with regarding what satisfaction, fulfillment, and happiness means to me:

Satisfaction: This is a feeling I get when I complete tasks. This experience is mainly functional in nature. It is solely based on the functional completion of a task at hand instead of emotional validation, impact, self-esteem, or confidence. Also, the tasks associated with this feeling lead to short-term goals and not lifelong aspirations. I experience satisfaction from performing tasks and providing deliverables to my clients based on the contractual terms we have agreed upon at the current market rate. Simply put, it results from getting fair financial compensation for utilizing my professional skills to deliver functional outcomes. If my compensation is lower than the market rate, I do not feel satisfied. If the tasks do not utilize my skills properly, I do not feel satisfied. Doing honest work, using my skills effectively, and supporting my family is how I feel satisfied.

Fulfillment: Delivering meaningful value and receiving unsolicited validation from someone I served are required for me to experience fulfillment. This is a level above satisfaction. There are elements of emotion, impact, and value required for fulfillment. This is not simply doing a job for fair compensation. I experience fulfillment when there is a deeper connection with my clients, students, or audience. It involves going beyond the simple, one-way delivery of content and reaching an authentic level of collaboration or a two-way sharing of experiences, feelings, thoughts, and reflections. The impact I deliver must be experienced, qualified, and validated by those I serve. The validation from my constituents is the only way I can be assured that the results from my work are truly impactful. As a parent and educator, I think the genuine validation from children and students is critical to keep us honest and growing. My 8-year-old son laughs at my poop jokes, so he thinks I am funny. However, everything that comes out of my mouth is considered to be "dad jokes" by my 14-year-old daughter. Therefore, she does not think I am funny. Who is right? Can both of my children be right? Can I be funny and not funny? Can both be true?

YES. I can be both. I am both. I do not get to decide whether I am funny or not. Only those who witness my "humor" are entitled to make that determination. This goes the same for other titles and attributes that we think we have in life. Am I a good spouse? Only my spouse can answer that. Am I a good parent? Only my children have the right to decide. Am I a good teacher? Only my students are qualified to make that determination. If you want to be effective and impactful, you must start by figuring out how those you serve define successful outcomes. Then work your butt off to make sure you deliver on what they want and need. When all it is said and done, the results of your work will speak for itself and your constituents will validate your work if you offer them the channel and opportunity to do so.

Happiness: This is the toughest one to crack. It seems so simple and yet it is so elusive. While satisfaction, fulfillment, and happiness are not always included together in people's criteria for success, when happiness is mentioned, everyone changes their criteria to include happiness. I have yet to meet anyone who was maxed out on their happiness capacity and could not handle another ounce of it. We all want to be happy and aspire to have more happiness in life. And yet, it is incredibly difficult to define what happiness is. It is almost impossible to measure it in a consistent way. As a strategist, I started with research first. I searched for any existing studies and data on happiness. I read, watched, and listened to everything I could find on the topic. While there was an abundance of big data and diverse perspectives, nothing really resonated with me. So, I moved onto my own primary research. I dug in deep to figure out what makes me happy. I was stumped by how difficult it was to answer this simple question, "What makes me happy?". Of course, the first answer that popped into my head was my family. But the obvious response was not good enough for me. What about my family makes me happy? Am I happy with their mere existence? Does everyone in my family make me happy? How broad or narrow of a definition should I use to define my family? This self-inflicted, tedious search led me to reflect on the moments I felt truly happy with my family. By reflecting on and validating the happy moments in my life, I was able to arrive at a definition. To me, happiness is an experience of pure bliss when I am not intellectually processing how happy I am at the moment. I am simply busy being happy. The acknowledgment and awareness of happiness usually comes after the fact through self-reflection.

When I was able to define and analyze satisfaction, fulfillment, and happiness based on my own life experience, I realized there is a linear relationship between these three attributes. I was able visualize this linear relationship by borrowing the conceptual model of Maslow's hierarchy of needs.

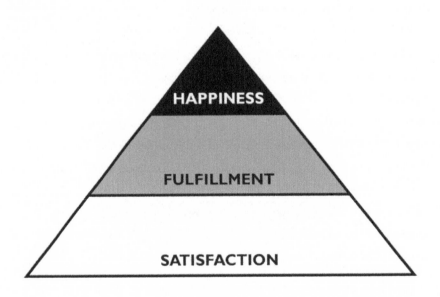

Satisfaction represents the fundamental level of meeting your basic needs in life, i.e. being fairly compensated for your work and being able to provide you and your family with shelter, food, clothing, and security. Nothing more. Once you have achieved satisfaction, you can start seeking fulfillment. Aspiring to deliver impact and value while you cannot feed yourself is an impossible task in the capitalist world that we live in. I have seen numerous nonprofits struggle with this as they fail to financially support their staff while they aspire to deliver meaningful impact in their community. If the staff cannot afford to pay their bills and support their families, how can they help anyone else? I am not questioning the mission or passion of those nonprofits. I am pointing out what seems to be a gap between reality and aspiration. This gap can also exist in individuals who want to make a difference in the world but lack the resources to take of themselves. While their passion is authentic and their mission is admirable, the likelihood of them delivering true impact is drastically reduced if they are living in their parents' basement and live off of their financial support. One cannot help others if one cannot help oneself first.

When you are striving for fulfillment, it is imperative to check your ego and embrace the marketer's mindset. By this I mean you must start by asking what are the needs of those you serve and gaining a deep understanding of what they say they want. Do not confuse this with what you want, what is important to you, or what you think their needs are. Remember, if no one thinks you're helpful, then you are not helpful, regardless of how helpful you think you are. Providing genuine value and receiving validation from those you impact will confirm if you're aligning your passions and desired mission.

By design, happiness sits above satisfaction and fulfillment on this pyramid. That is because happiness should be pure and cherished. It must not be diluted or compromised. It must be protected. If not, you will have to deal with the inevitable disappointment, confusion, and stress of unhappiness. A wide-reaching grasp for happiness does not help. Instead, having a narrow, precise, and authentic definition of happiness will effectively guide you to achieving the happiness that you seek. Shortcuts or settling for second-best will only disappoint you. Remember that you deserve the best.

A strategic mental model is great but it is only the starting point. In order to be successful, you must create a thorough tactical plan. A strategy without a tactical plan and effective implementation is nothing more than wishful thinking. Happiness is too important to simply exist as wishful thinking.

Why Life ROI?

I had to figure out a tactical plan to implement and test my strategy for achieving happiness in my own life. While my brain was deep in analytical and linear-thinking mode, a random TV commercial caught my attention. The commercial was for a financial services firm. A well-groomed and somewhat academic-looking financial advisor was having a "genuine" conversation with his client. They were talking about what she wanted to do in retirement and how the financial firm's services could help her achieve her dream a lot sooner. The financial advisor used the line "Why wait?" in his pitch. That struck a chord with me as I was reminded of my close call in 2016. There is no guarantee on how long we all will live. None of our birth certificates come with an expiration date. I got lucky in 2016, but Dan didn't. He didn't wake up that morning knowing it would be his last. None of us know when it will be our last day. So, the thought of waiting until you have a certain amount of money to do what makes you happy seemed ridiculous.

There is an abundance of clichés about the scarcity of life. Every culture has them. One of the most popular clichés in the U.S. is "time is your most valuable asset." When I read this, my train of thought immediately goes down the track of asset, investment, margin, and return on investment (ROI). That led me to google "Life ROI." Unsurprisingly, a few of the search results containing both terms were for financial services firms. The language around "Life ROI" was all about financial planning for the golden years of retirement. I know that the term return on investment is firmly rooted in finance, but I couldn't keep myself from wondering what would a pragmatic ROI model look like for life?

This led me to first establish the following fundamental premises on which to build my hypothesis for Life ROI:

- Time is your most valuable asset.
- Time is the micro unit of measurement over a period, which results in the singular macro unit of life.
- Therefore, time and life are one.
- How we spend our time ultimately determines the quality of our life.
- How we spend our time ultimately determines the success of our life.
- Time is the ultimate unit of measurement that is truly universal.
- Every human on Earth has the exact same access to 24 hours every day.
- One cannot buy or trade for more time.
- Regardless of education, wealth, age, gender, power, race, or sexual orientation, one cannot squeeze in more than 24 hours a day.
- Time is the greatest equalizer for humankind.
- Time must be the unit of measurement used to calculate Life ROI.

If we assume, we work an 8-hour workday, sleep 8 hours per doctors' recommendation, it leaves 8 hours in our day that go unaccounted for. Most of us are either physically in the office working or schedule work activities on our calendar so we have some record of how the 16 hours are spent in our day. However, the remaining 8 hours are spent on mundane daily activities like errands, eating, commuting, shower, etc. We simply do not track these 8 hours. On weekends, it may be as many as 16 hours that go unaccounted for. Collectively, up to 45% of our most valuable asset is unaccounted for on a monthly basis. Our time simply slips through our fingers. This was simply insane to me. I had to find an effective way to track and measure how we spend and invest our most valuable asset.

After arriving at this realization, I went on to research how life and time are measured. I began by looking at all the things that we track and measure today: the amount of money we make, money we spend, water we drink, steps we take, calories we consume, etc. I could not find anything meaningful in terms of how we track and measure our time. I assume a majority of working professionals and students use some type of calendar, app, or planner to keep track of the things they have to do in the future. Some of us may use them to plan vacations and special events. However, I would guess that none of us use them as a tool for reflection and to gauge how we spend our time. We might often ask ourselves, "Where did the last week/month/year go?" If we honestly believe that time is our most valuable asset, how and why do we so readily and repeatedly lose track of it? I don't know many people who would so nonchalantly and repeatedly be ok with not knowing where their paycheck, savings, or investments went. All of us would be outraged or terribly distressed if we didn't know where our money was. Then why is it that we are completely passive and dismissive about our most valuable asset?

Perhaps one of the reasons why is in the word we use to describe the activity itself. Strictly from a business perspective, cash-spending activities are recorded as expenses on a Profit and Loss statement. Nobody likes expenses, especially entrepreneurs like myself. Expenses quickly add up, even though they are necessary to operate and grow a business. The majority of expenses are spent to address short-term needs and transactions. When we make investments, though, the objective is more long-term and strategic. Instead of focusing on the short-term costs, we focus on the relational, sustainable, and scalable outcomes. We do not treat investments the same way we treat expenses. Sustainable success can only be achieved if there is a balance between short-term, transactional expenses and long-term, strategic investments. Each business must figure it out based on its own unique challenges and opportunities. Borrowing this perspective from the business world, the question we should all ask ourselves as individuals is how much of our time is simply spent versus strategically invested. What percentage of your daily 24 hours are you spending away versus intentionally investing to achieve long-term success? Are we operating from a place of harmonized management of our assets? Or are we allowing our most precious asset to slip through our fingers every day, week, month, and year? Unlike businesses, most people do not keep an accurate log of how much time we spend or invest. Businesses can count their cash on hand, available line of credit, inventory assets, and fixed and non-operating assets. We cannot count up how much time we have left. There is no way of knowing how much of our most valuable asset we have in supply. Therefore, I think we should all operate with a sense of urgency, not in terms of rushing through life, but in terms of clarity. The sooner we figure out what we want out of life, define success, create a clear strategy, and implement an actionable plan to achieve it, the sooner we will feel true happiness. Like the financial advisor said in the commercial, "Why wait?"

Once I was able to define satisfaction, fulfillment, and happiness as my attributes of success, I decided to start my quest to define the formula for Life ROI. I started with happiness because it is the most important of the three. The first task was figuring out how to go about measuring happiness. As an entrepreneur and business school professor, I like to measure things. As a Korean-American, math has always been a familiar and comfortable language to me. I combined my affinity for metrics and math to prove my Life ROI hypothesis and put it into practice. Here is what made sense to me. These are the main components of the happiness:

T = TIME
A = ACTIVITY
P = PEOPLE
E = ENVIRONMENT

As I was reflecting on the happy moments of my life, every happy memory included these components. Not all four were present in every instance but various combinations of these components were always present. So, the following set of equations seem logical to me:

HAPPINESS = T (A + P + E)
HAPPINESS = T (A + P)
HAPPINESS = T (A + E)
HAPPINESS = T (P + E)

I am happy when my family and I watch movies together in the theater, especially those theaters with reclining chairs: T (A + P + E). In this example, watching movies is the activity, my family is the people, and the movie theater is the environment. I am just as happy when we are watching a movie in a place with less comfortable chairs, like our basement: T (A + P). Happiness can still be achieved without the component of environment when the components of activity and people remain consistent. Anyone busy with working, raising children, nurturing relationships, and caring for older family members can probably resonate with this next example. Happiness can be achieved by engaging in an activity by yourself, for yourself, and in one's favorite environment. When our days are filled with caring for and serving others, we often forget to care for ourselves. Self-care has become more popular and arguably more important in the last few years. For a Gen Xer like myself, self-care is quite difficult to adopt. I grew up watching my parents make painful and selfless sacrifices. They were especially selfless, as many immigrant parents are. I do not recall my parents ever complaining about their work being meaningless, feeling unfulfilled, or longing for self-care. They worked 16-hour days, seven days a week, drenched in sweat, tears, and racist harassments. And yet I do not remember hearing a single complaint from them. Here I am, crying about not feeling fulfilled at work and whining about not having enough self-care in my life, drenched in privilege. I told my mom how each generation seems to be getting weaker and weaker. I compared myself to her when she was my age, when she sacrificed so much of herself for my sister and me. I told her I felt ashamed for how weak I felt compared to her. She rebutted with a surprising perspective. She said our struggles are simply different, not more or less, tougher or easier. She didn't think she could do what I was doing when she was my age.

"Your father and I sacrificed so you and your sister would not have to struggle as we did," she said. "It was our duty as parents to do all that we could to support our children. Although we embraced our duty with pride, we didn't have many choices when it came down to it. As immigrants, we did what we could so you could have choices. Do not waste them. Do not let our sacrifices go to waste by not taking advantage of the choices and opportunities we worked so hard for you to have."

I never looked at it that way. I always felt too guilty to take time for myself. I thought that self-care was a privilege and a luxury for people who are weak and selfish. How dare I, the son of hard-working immigrants, to engage in such frivolous acts of selfishness! My mom's words set me straight, though, with unconditional and authentic love. I realized I am no good to anyone if I am miserable, or even worse, dead. Working my ass off without any self-care led me to that evening in Seattle back in 2016. The last person I expected to learn about self-care from was my mom. I needed to distinguish positive motivation and guilt within my inner dialog. There is nothing honorable about working myself to death, especially when my parents have already done that to provide choices and opportunities at something better. My parents' sacrifices provided the platform for me to create fulfillment and happiness for my family while allowing me the opportunities to find fulfillment and happiness for myself. It enabled me to get grounded and better myself as well as others in my life through experiences, relationships, and our environment.

These reflections and revelations have inspired me to pursue a deeper understanding of Life ROI. Not just because it will better my life but also because I sincerely believe it will better the lives of my family, friends, students, and clients, both directly and indirectly. For the first time in my life, I have found my calling. Working on Life ROI sharpens my skills, feeds my passion, challenges my fears, deepens my thinking, and focuses my intentions to the most important thing: life.

I look forward to sharing the Life ROI framework I have created and have been practicing with you in the upcoming chapters. I sincerely hope it will be worth the investment of your time to read the remainder of this book.

P.S. I have received feedback from truly mathematically gifted people who have said that these equations do not really equal happiness; rather, they yield happiness. They are absolutely correct. I looked into yield formulas and I could not make sense of them, so I am sticking with my original equations for now. I guess I am not as mathematically gifted as I had thought. I hope I don't get my Asian membership card revoked.

Life ROI Framework: Research

360 Perception Survey

All strategy work begins with research. The research must be thorough, methodical, focused, and relevant in order for the overall strategy to be successful. Designing and conducting research on oneself is not a common concept. "Finding myself" may be a popular cliché, but implementing analytical research on oneself with strategic focus is not widely practiced.

The Life ROI framework starts with conducting a comprehensive 360 research on ourselves. Similar to 360 performance reviews and comprehensive marketing research, we are seeking data on how others in our lives perceive us and what position we own in this world. This research requires you to practice vulnerability and bravery with clear intentions. I would like to take a moment to explain my perspective on the topic of vulnerability. I am not asking you to be vulnerable. To me, being vulnerable means leaving yourself wide open as an easy target for whoever wants to take a shot. It sounds terrifying. It reminds me of my early days in New York City. I do not wish that on you. That's not what is required to do this research. Instead, I am asking you to practice vulnerability. You are in full control of how much vulnerability you want to practice and with whom. You should also practice with clear intentions of gathering relevant and meaningful data on the most important subject in life: you.

The first step in this 360 research is to identify who you want to invite to participate in this research on your behalf. The people you invite will be asked to answer questions about you that are intimate and transparent in nature. The amount of people that participate is not as important as the depth of intimacy and respect you have for each other. This is qualitative research. Having 10 or more participants can provide greater breadth and depth to your data, but it is not required. There is no correlation between a higher number of participants and a higher quality of research outcomes.

Begin the selection process by categorizing the people in your life into two categories: professional and personal. People from your professional life can include current and former supervisors, colleagues, direct reports, clients, vendors, partners, and mentors. You don't have to include someone for each title for the sake of covering them all. However, each person should have an established level of intimacy and trust with you to be included in this research. Unfortunately, people with fixed-mindsets may perceive your intentional practice of vulnerability as a weakness and may use it against you. Only include professional contacts that you trust and have shared experiences with. If you have even an ounce of doubt about a certain individual, do not include him or her. It is not worth the professional risk.

People from your personal life can include immediate and extended family members; friends from childhood, high school, college, work, and special interest groups; current and former significant others; spouses; and children (preferably teens or older). This category is much broader and deeper than the first. Our family members, from parents and siblings to children, can provide unique perspectives from multiple generations. If you are close with your grandparents and they played an important role in your upbringing, please include them. Grandparents not only can provide a sage perspective, but they also have a completely different view of you than your parents. While parents are focused on your safety, knowledge, discipline, and day-to-day upbringing, grandparents can provide wisdom, long-term life lessons, and unconditional encouragement that is different from that of your parents. Our friends also know us differently based on when the friendship was established and what you went through together. Your friends from childhood can provide a very different perspective than your friends from adulthood or work. Even though the timing between high school and college is immediate and sequential, friends from each stage may see you differently because we all go through such major developmental changes during these years. Your current partner and spouse must be included in this research, while former significant others are completely optional. Include them at your own risk!

Once you have selected and qualified both professional and personal participants, gather their email addresses and set up an online questionnaire on your favorite survey tool or platform. It doesn't matter which tool or platform you use, as long as it can cover the basic requirements for this research survey: the ability to offer anonymous responses to ensure authentic feedback and the ability to distribute, manage, sort, and export reports from multiple participants.

> *Please use the following worksheet in The Life ROI Workbook to complete this step of the framework:* RESEARCH | Survey Participants Worksheet

Please note that the professional and personal participants you have selected for the 360 research are to be considered as your personal brand ambassadors. Let's review the questions you will be asking them to answer on your behalf. (You will also be answering these questions yourself!) The questions are listed in sequential order and designed to start on a broad level and dive deeper and deeper as the questionnaire progresses. There are two versions for each question for external and internal evaluations.

Question 1:

- <u>Internal</u>: What are my top strengths? Please list up to three strengths.
- <u>External</u>: What do you think are my top strengths? Please list up to three strengths.

This opening question is the easiest to answer for both you and your participants because it is positive in nature and inviting. Hopefully, you will not have any difficulty answering this question for yourself. If you do, you may find possible causes for your difficulty in the "Inner Voices" exercise later on in the section.

Question 2:

- <u>Internal</u>: In what areas can I improve? Please list up to three areas of development.
- <u>External</u>: In what areas can I improve? Please list up to three areas of development.

This question is tougher than the first but, hopefully, its focus on constructive criticism and growth makes it easier to provide a transparent response. Brutally honest answers are more helpful than polite ones.

Question 3:

- <u>Internal</u>: When was the last time I was at my happiest? Please describe the occasion and the circumstances.
- <u>External</u>: When was the last time you saw me at my happiest? Please describe the occasion and the circumstances.

Question 4:

- <u>Internal</u>: When was the last time I was stressed out? Please describe the occasion and the circumstances.
- <u>External</u>: When was the last time you saw me stressed out? Please describe

the occasion and the circumstances.

Responses for these two questions will typically paint scenes out of a movie called "Your Life." Most answers should include when it was, where you were, who you were with, what you were doing, why they thought you were happy or stressed, and any context to validate their observation. The more details, the better. However, it may be difficult for you to think about the last time you were at your happiest. While it can be easier to recall the last time you were stressed, it is more difficult to recollect when we were truly happy. This is because when we experience happiness, we do not typically interrupt the joyful moment to analytically assess whether we are experiencing happiness or not. If you do stop to analyze it, you are often taken out of the moment or you stop enjoying it because you are thinking. When we experience true happiness, we must be 100% committed and engaged with whatever is causing it. I believe happiness is later acknowledged in our reflection, when we think back to specific moments, talk with our loved ones about specific events, and go through old photos and videos of times spent doing something worthy of documenting. I also know it is beneficial to reflect on a daily basis to acknowledge and appreciate those special moments that happen every day (i.e. a gratitude practice). These questions motivated me to practice daily gratitude and reflection to acknowledge, appreciate, change, and improve upon everything I do and everything that happens to me.

Question 5:
- Internal: In which environment or situation do I think I am at my best? Please describe the occasion and the circumstances.
- External: In which environment or situation do you think I am at my best? Please describe your observation or experience.

Answers to this question can both validate and contradict where and how your areas of strength are being practiced. Do your professional and personal environments allow you to properly and effectively leverage your strengths? Or do they encourage (and sometimes force) you to develop in new ways so that you can be effective? Just like Questions 3 and 4, detailed responses can provide meaningful and relevant context to where, when, how, why, and with whom you are at your best.

Question 6:

- Internal: If I were to make a highlight reel on my life, what one scene would I make sure to include?
- External: If you were to make a highlight reel on my life, what one scene would you make sure to include?

This is 100% an exercise in reflection. Regardless of how old you are, what are the major milestones that you accomplished or challenges you experienced? What did you make happen or what happened to you that shaped who you are today? It does not have to be a happy moment. It just has to be significant to make it into your highlight reel.

Question 7:

- Internal: Which popular consumer brand do I associate with myself (e.g. Nike, Apple, Gatorade, Toyota, etc.)? Which of the brand's attributes remind me of myself?
- External: Which popular consumer brand do you associate with me (e.g. Nike, Apple, Gatorade, Toyota, etc.)? Which of the brand's attributes remind you of me?

This question is designed to reveal and assess your character attributes through a non-personal comparison. Some people may find it difficult to pick a brand because they may struggle to find a connection between products/services and a human being. However, those who can name a brand and identify the attributes will provide you with valuable perspectives. This is the first of three questions designed to ease participants into providing more in-depth responses.

Question 8:

- Internal: How would I like to have someone I know describe me in one sentence to someone who does not know me?
- External: How would you describe me in one sentence to someone who does not know me?

This one sentence should be considered your personal brand's tagline. This is what your personal brand ambassadors think of you and how they will describe and promote you when you are not present.

Question 9:

- Internal: What ONE word would I choose to describe myself? Why have I chosen this word for myself?
- External: What ONE word would you choose to describe me? Why have you chosen this word for me?

As a brand strategist, the most critical part of my job is to identify, define, and create the brand's DNA, or the true essence of the brand on a nuclear level. When all the distraction, noise, and BS is removed, what is the one sticky, gooey, most flavorful ingredient left at the bottom of the pot? This question is designed to draw out your personal brand values. Answers to this question represent how your personal brand ambassadors will describe the essence of the life you lead and the legacy you will leave behind. When you are long gone, this is how your loved ones will remember you and miss you.

Question 10:

- Internal: Is there anything I would like to add to my life that may be currently missing?
- External: Is there anything you would like to see me add to my life that may

be currently missing?

Unlike some animals, our eyes are designed to look forward from the front of our face. This means that humans' field of vision spans about 120 degrees of arc. For Asians like myself, it may be closer to 300 degrees with peripheral vision (just kidding, I hope you are not offended by me poking fun at my own stereotype). Regardless, it is a fact that we cannot see 360 degrees around ourselves. We have limited vision to what's generally in front of us. Therefore, this question is designed to borrow our personal brand ambassadors' perspectives to see what we cannot see ourselves. This question is also the last question in the 360 research questionnaire. It is designed to leave participants in a place of aspirational and forward thinking.

> *Please use the following worksheet in The Life ROI Workbook to complete this step of the framework:* RESEARCH | Survey Questions: External & Internal

All responses to this questionnaire will be thoroughly evaluated during the analysis phase.

Defining Moments

When Hollywood depicts a person facing an imminent life-or-death moment, they often see moments from their life flash before their eyes, like a highlight reel. Some of these moments are bound to be joyful experiences and difficult challenges that they overcame. Reflecting on my 48 years, I have been blessed with many happy moments. However, the majority of my growth has come during and after difficult times. The greater the difficulties, the greater the lessons learned. I have already shared some of my most challenging, impactful, and defining moments in earlier chapters. These not-so-pleasant experiences largely shaped who I am today and how I face each new day, experience, relationship, and challenge.

Coming to the U.S. as a 13-year-old boy, deep in the instability of puberty, was a defining moment for me on multiple levels. The days and years that followed challenged me at my core as my world was turned upside down. I had to continually engage in a fight-or-flight response to simply survive. The grit and hustle built into my DNA were developed and amplified in these early years, which I greatly benefit from as an entrepreneur. As an outsider, separated by language and culture, I was forced to simply observe from the sidelines. Trying to read nonverbal cues like body language, facial expressions, physical reactions, and mannerisms helped me to develop holistic communication skills. Whether I am consulting, teaching, speaking, conversing, or parenting, my keen observation of words, body language, decisions, and behaviors helps me predict what may come next with a higher level of probability.

Unexpectedly losing my father defined how I want to approach the rest of my life, however long it may be. For as long as I can remember, I wanted more from my father and wished he was different, even though I didn't really know what I wanted from him. I was quick to judge and complain about his incompetency as a father. My animosity toward my father peaked when I turned 30 and saw him not just as my father but also as a man. I asked myself this question one day, "If I had met my father just as another man under different circumstances, would I want to grab a beer with him?" Based on our differences in personality, my answer was no. I was disappointed, and I blamed him for it. I was so ignorant and hateful, unfairly judging him from my limited experience as a man and husband. I had yet to become a father myself, yet I was handing out tickets for my father's behavior like a seasoned parking enforcement officer in midtown Manhattan.

My period of deep thinking and reflection after my son was born led me to adopt a completely new perspective. I was finally able to hear what my mom has been telling me for years.

"Your father is doing his best based on what he knows," she would say. "He doesn't know what he doesn't know."

He grew up with a father who may have been physically around but was never emotionally there for him. My father did not know how to emotionally be there for me because he himself had never experienced it. He did the best he could with what he knew and had.

I never took the chance to own up to my mistakes and reconcile with my father. I thought about the day when I would kneel in front of him and beg for his forgiveness. But when opportunities came, I simply waived them off for "later," which of course never happened. My father could not wait around for my ideal moment. Life does not wait for anything or anyone. It flows and keeps going whether you are ready or not. There is never an ideal time or place to do the right thing. Now is as perfect as it gets. Procrastination leads to future regrets that will yield a lifetime of guilt.

Experiencing my own life-or-death moment also served as the catalyst for my work on the Life ROI framework and this book. As cliché as it may be, facing the end of something you cherish forces you to appreciate it more than ever before (sometimes for the first time). Luckily for me, I was given a second chance to make sure I not only cherish my life but also maximize it to the fullest.

All of us have multiple defining moments in life. However, only some of us reflect, recognize, and acknowledge these defining moments. I have consulted, taught, mentored, and spoken to thousands of people. I have met only two people who said that they have never experienced any challenges and could not identify any defining moments. On one hand, they may be lucky enough to have avoided tragedies, difficulties, and challenges. On the other hand, I sincerely hope that their lucky streak continues for the remainder of their lives. Otherwise, they may be devastatingly unprepared for a massive sledgehammer of hard life lessons coming their way.

I invite you to look back on your life and reflect on the paths, hills, valleys, peaks, and pitfalls you traveled through to get to where you are today. Reflect on those moments you wished could last forever and the moments you wished could disappear forever. Who and what created those moments? How did you get through those hard minutes, hours, days, months, or years when you didn't think it was possible? How have you survived and thrived on your journey so far? What defining moments shaped and strengthened your values? What lessons did you learn during your ascents and falls? It is impossible to predict the future. However, when we study our history, especially our personal history, we can build up a lasting confidence to lead us into our future with greater certainty.

Inner Voices

In the days and months after blacking out in Seattle, my mind became cluttered with voices, thoughts, and images of my imminent death. My inner voice would whisper, "You got lucky back in 2016. But your luck is going to run out today. This is it. You better not drive your kids to school because you will take them out with you when you crash your car." Then an image of mine and my children's lifeless, bloody bodies would flash inside my head. Sometimes, I would find myself driving away from my typical route toward a highway because I heard, "You'd better not take the highway home, or you will crash into multiple cars and kill innocent people."

These inner voices and horrific omens became louder and more frequent as time passed.

As I was driving to a meeting one day, Radiolab started playing on the radio. The episode was called "Voices in Your Head" and it immediately caught my attention. For the next 15 minutes, I became completely immersed in the program. I arrived at my destination but remained in my car to listen to the rest of the episode. The first thing that struck me was that I was not alone; others hear voices in their heads, too. This is not weird. I do not need to be admitted to a mental institution or put on medication. I felt so relieved. One of the featured experts on the show said that these voices aren't ours. They are the voices of those who impacted us during our impressionable years growing up, both positively and negatively. These voices live on in our heads for a long time, so we begin to think they are our own but they are not. We simply become used to listening to them. Goosebumps popped up all over my body. I frantically started thinking about whose voices were living inside my head. Especially the ones that predicted my death every day. It took me weeks of investigative reflection and questioning to identify the source of this voice of doom. What I discovered was that this voice did not exist before I arrived in New York City back in 1984. Also, this was a collective voice from all those who spewed hate, slurs, and violence toward me.

"Dirty chink!"
"Stupid chink!"
"Get the fuck out, chink!"
"Go back to China!"
"You don't belong here!"

Prior to 1984, the word "chink" occupied zero space in my mind and heart. Needless to say, within weeks of arriving in New York City, it became a trigger word that activated my fight-or-flight response. "Chink" consumed my rational and empathetic nature, replacing them with a violent and volatile lava of resentment.

These voices evolved to include the subtler micro aggressions and underhanded comments from my professional years later in life.

"Well, I can't promote you because English is not your first language and I could tell you still don't have a full grasp on it yet."

"Your work is descent enough to put in front of clients, but I can't have you present it. You don't have a business degree so I don't think you can pull it off."

"The reason why you were hired is because the founder of the company felt bad about what he did to your people during the Korean War."

Over the years, these external voices morphed into a singular internal voice, spewing doubt, insecurity, guilt, fear, and hate. This voice also found an effective tool to attack me. Because I am a visual person, this voice would use alarming and terrifying images to get through to me. Sometimes, I would physically shake my head to get rid of these vivid and realistic images.

Acknowledging, defining, and confronting these voices did not silence them, though. They continued their campaign of fear for months after I blacked out. I had to find an effective and sustainable away to deal with them. In fact, they became louder when I tried to ignore them. I spoke with people I knew who had experienced trauma and difficult challenges in life. I wanted to learn about how they coped with their own struggles. After multiple conversations, I decided to go back to where it started and go through everything I did in the days leading up the incident in Seattle. I decided to face my demons by recreating the scene at the same restaurant and table on the same day exactly a year later. I planned it all out; I would travel to Seattle on June 27, 2017, visit the same destinations, and repeat the same activities as I had done the year before. As soon as I booked the airline ticket to go back to Seattle, my internal voice of doom became louder than it had ever been before. It began making very specific predictions.

"You will crash and die on your way to Denver International Airport, so you won't even make it onto the flight."

"Your plane will crash on your way to Seattle."

"You'd better have your wife check in with your Airbnb host the next morning, because they will find your cold, dead body in bed."

"Your return flight to Denver will crash in the Rockies and you will never make it back home."

I decided to journal and record every step of my trip to help me face my fear and prove that my inner voice's predictions were wrong. Here are my actual journal entries that I saved on my phone in 2017:

Tuesday, 6/27

5:03 AM: To the voice that whispered I would never make it to Seattle again because I would get into a car crash on my way to the airport due to fatigue from sleeping only an hour and half... I just parked in the economy lot and walked into the airport. You are owned.

10:58 AM: To the voice that said the plane would go down and it would have been the first and the last flight since my blackout... the plane landed safely and the only deadly part of the flight was the stench of the deli meat the guy in the aisle seat next to me was eating. Death in plane crash owned.

12:59 PM: Because the restaurant where my blackout happened no longer serves fish tacos, I had some at the beach that mom and I were supposed to visit last year a few hours before the incident happened. Fish tacos owned.

Wednesday, 6/28

9:52 AM: To the voice that told me I would die in my sleep and nobody would discover my dead body until the owners of my Airbnb came in after my checkout time... I woke up with my heart still beating. 364 days owned to face my 365th day since the black out.

12:40 PM: Arrived at Stone House restaurant exactly one year to the date. The patio looks smaller and different than I remember. There are four ladies sitting at the table I sat at last year. They have gift bags on the table. They may take a while and the restaurant will close their lunch service in an hour. I tell the waitress why I am here and she is ok with me asking them to switch tables. I put on my best smile and tell the ladies what happened and why I am here. They are more than understanding and willing to accommodate my unusual request. One of the older ladies, who is an Asian-American, tells me she is also a retired nurse. What?! Is this the most popular spot for retired nurses in this neighborhood? What are the chances of one retired nurse saving my life a year ago and another granting me my strange request a year later?

As I sit and begin staring at the exact spot where I blacked out, my heart starts racing and my eyes well up. I did not expect this — not this much, not this deep, and not this quick. I had to put my sunglasses back on. They don't serve fish tacos anymore, so I order fish and chips (close enough). I do my best to remember the exact beer that I ordered but can't, so I ask for help from the waitress. I order the same Pale Ale. The first sip brings me back quite suddenly and unexpectedly. My heart feels heavy now, and the back of my neck feels stiff and I feel a headache coming on. I am scared all over again. Did the beer cause this? Do I have some insane allergy to one of the ingredients? Or the way the beer was brewed?

Ridiculous! I am going to have another sip and own this. The second sip makes it worse. I back off and start drinking more water. The beer is not worth it. I want to walk out of here... but on my own this time. The fish and chips were excellent but my emotions killed my appetite. I ate most of the fish and just a few bites of fries. The waitress was very helpful with putting in the dessert orders for the kind ladies who moved their celebration over to another table. She shares that one of them ordered bread pudding. I ask for four bread puddings for the rest of the table. I figure the lady who enjoys bread pudding can take it home with her if the others prefer different desserts.

I click away with the camera on my phone, trying to capture every inch and angle of the place where it happened. I try to figure out the exact spot where I fell over and where my head landed, which was next to the table where that retired nurse was having dinner. I partially close my eyes and try visualizing myself on the ground. My eyes well up again. While I stare at the spot, I notice there is a tiny sliver of green popping up through the gaps of brick pavement. It looks like a plant, probably a type of weed. I never imagined a weed could be so beautiful. This one is absolutely gorgeous. It is approximately where my left hand would have been and where that nurse would have kneeled, holding my hand and asking me to squeeze back. Is this a sign? A simple coincidence? The weed is still beautiful, regardless.

I can't eat another bite as the fish now tastes bitter and seems to have grown sharp thorns. I ask for the check. The waitress delivers it with a smile and praises me for buying dessert for the ladies. It's the least I can do for the ladies for accommodating my strange request. I take a couple more photos, this time at ground level. I go over to thank the ladies again for their kindness. They wish me the best. I visit the restroom I meant to last year before driving to visit another friend. But that bathroom stop never happened last year. As I walk out of the restaurant, the ladies harmoniously thank me for the dessert as the waitress had brought it out. Damn it. I wanted it to happen after I left. I thank them again and walk across the street to the rental car.

As I sit at the steering wheel, I feel sharp pains on the back of my neck, upper shoulder, and my chest. The headache is now full-blown. I lower the window and take one more parting photo of the restaurant. Perhaps I want to capture an evidential shot of myself walking away from this place alive. To that voice that haunted me for the past 365 days, I am walking away from here alive. I sat, ate, drank, thought, felt, cried, pained, and reflected, and now I am driving away alive. Fuck you!

Thursday, 6/29

10:51 PM: Although I have not heard the voice since Wednesday, for the record, my plane has landed safely.

Friday, 6/30

1:19 AM: After an unscheduled stop to pick up some homegrown vegetables from my mom's friend on my way home from the airport, I drive with the sunroof open, breathing in fresh mile-high air that is unusually humid. It feels like more than just air. My lungs fill up with tranquility, warmth, energy, and life. As I cross the familiar intersection just minutes from my mom's place, the sky opens up with thunderous rainfall. It seems like my inner voice of doom ordered this downfall in its last pathetic attempt to carry out its prediction. I chuckle as I drive through it. When I get to my mom's place, she puts out a spread of familiar and unconditional love. I dig in to fill up my soul with her love. After sharing an edited recap of the trip with my mom, I mistakenly open up about the inner voice of doom. The horror on her face should have been expected. I immediately start to regret saying anything. I quickly pivot to tell her that the voice is all gone now. It has been absent (or at least super quiet) since Wednesday. I can't be sure if they are completely gone, but they sure are quiet. I am now where I belong as I sit on my beat-up old couch, writing my final entry on this journey. I am back where I am loved, where I serve a purpose, and where I live. Live on, I will.

365 days done.

June 28th owned.

Voice of doom owned.

Fuck you!

The voice of doom quieted down after my return visit to Seattle. It would try coming back here and there, but for the most part, it sat in the corner quietly. I thought I owned it completely until April 2019. It came back with a vengeance, equipped with a new deadly weapon.

After shutting down MetroBoom and filing for bankruptcy, I took on consulting and teaching work wherever I could find it. A former student introduced me to Centura Health, which led me to a one-year consulting engagement. (Thank you, Chip Neilson!) Then a successful American-Australian entrepreneur invited me to teach at The Centre for Entrepreneurial Research and Innovation (CERI) which he founded in Perth, Australia. (Thank you, Charlie Bass!) I was able to bring my family along, including my mom, and we enjoyed our first international family vacation. While I had spurts of financial stability and accomplishment, I still needed to decide what to do next. One day, Alexis asked me a question. I knew she had been thinking about it for years, and how tough it was for Alexis to ask me this question, "Will you ever consider getting a job again?"

Alexis is the exact opposite of me when it comes to risk and stability. My risk tolerance is high and I do not need stability. Alexis is risk-averse and needs stability in her life. She grounds me when I start to chase unicorns and search for a Leprechaun's pot of gold. Knowing what it took for Alexis to ask this question, I promised her that I had already been searching for, and will continue to work toward finding, a job. I had to explain to her how unemployable and undesirable entrepreneurs are to potential employers. Even though the thought of working in the same cubicle every day, answering to some incompetent boss, succumbing to bureaucracy, and paddling into the swamp of office politics and personal insecurities felt suffocating to me, I knew I have to do what is best for my family. I had robbed my family of financial stability and quality family time while I was chasing my entrepreneurial dreams. They sacrificed and suffered from the sidelines, especially Alexis. The spouses and partners of entrepreneurs often suffer in silence, feeling helpless as they watch their counterparts struggle in their self-initiated entrepreneurial shitstorms.

After countless rejections, I finally landed a job. A trusted friend referred me to an organization she had been with since its conception. I was grateful for the opportunity, as well as for her trust and support. Everyone I met in the organization was friendly and welcoming. I especially liked the president, who fought to hire me, and my supervisor whom I got to spend quality time with while attending a 10-day training session abroad. Contrary to my reservations, I began to think I could actually enjoy having a job again. The camaraderie and sense of belonging were fantastic. Unfortunately, my optimistic outlook did not last long. Within weeks, the president was fired. It was poorly packaged and presented as an "amicable separation," but I have been around the block too many times to buy that BS. A few months later, my supervisor, who I respected professionally and liked personally, was also fired by the new leadership. While I tried to maintain hope for myself for the sake of providing stability for my family, I knew what was about to happen.

In the months leading up to that day in April, I shared my prediction with a few close colleagues. Most of them waved it off, and one of them even said I was building a self-fulfilling prophecy in my head. Under the passive-aggressive, inexperienced, incapable, and privileged new leadership, short cuts were encouraged to meet the bottom numbers, sacrificed the wellbeing of the constituents we served, and accountability was dismissed. I could not quietly sit by and watch these disgraceful acts, so I spoke up when necessary. I quickly became the thorn in the side of those who were willing to forego integrity and jeopardize the safety of our constituents for the sake of meeting the bottom line.

In the beginning of 2019, the perfect enforcer was hired to begin the brutal process of instilling fear throughout the organization and cleaning house. She also became my supervisor. The arrangement was perfect for the passive-aggressive leadership who didn't want to do her own dirty work. The first act of sabotage came on April 3rd. I had a meeting to update my new supervisor, who was the newly hired enforcer. It was clear to me that she had her own agenda. Halfway through the meeting, she hijacked the conversation. She began laying down the first step of her plan to set me up. She made accusations against me based on assumptions, and I tried to defend myself. I assured her that I had the documentation to prove her wrong. It was clear that she wasn't ready for this type of response, so she resorted to the old "it doesn't matter, you have to do as I tell you to, anyway" tactic. It is interesting how egotistical, insecure, and narcissistic individuals think they are somehow smarter than everyone else when their tactics are always so shallow and painfully obvious. These individuals also believe they are invincible, creating their own versions of the truth and leveraging their position of power to manufacture deception and fear to serve themselves. She obnoxiously typed away on her laptop while we talked. It seemed she was taking copious notes so she could use it later to distort the truth and serve her own agenda. There would be more sabotages to come. This was just the beginning. She was also a loud type, which only amplified her narcissism. Bringing the truth to light always trumps these self-serving, deceitful, and fear-driven acts, though. Her explicit orders also violated the organization's standard practice and HR policies against putting an employee under duress. I recorded the entire conversation on my phone. The truth was on my side.

I walked out of that meeting and called Alexis. I told her about the intentional act of sabotage that just happened, which we both had expected. I told her my plan was to resign the next day, and she supported my decision, as she has always done. It is a blessing to have someone in your life who has your back in good times and bad. I sought the professional opinion of a seasoned HR expert and friend to ensure that I had a valid case of discrimination and resignation under duress. She confirmed that I did and provided me with methodical steps to resign with professionalism and dignity.

The next day, I closely followed every step advised by my HR friend. I met with the organization's HR manager to submit my resignation under duress and explain the circumstances leading to that decision. She asked if I had another job lined up, and I told her no. Then she asked if I had enough savings to last me and my family until I land another job. I told her we had enough saved to pay our mortgage for three months. She was surprised by my answer. I could tell she was genuinely concerned for my and my family's wellbeing. I explained how I could not consider myself a person of integrity if I only practiced it when it is convenient. Integrity is not conditional in my book. Integrity must be practiced at all times, especially when you have something to lose. I could not go through another day of deceit, fear, and narcissism that forces me to compromise my values. No amount of money can justify not being able to look into my children's eyes because I compromised my values and integrity. She asked if I would like severance, and I refused. I explained how the organization had a history of providing severance in exchange for people's silence and cooperation via air-tight non-disclosure agreements (NDA). Why would a small, start-up organization make it standard practice to offer severance in exchange for signing an NDA if there is nothing to hide? I operated my own businesses for years, and I never attempted to buy the silence of a former staff member. I would rather uphold the truth and ethical business practices. I thanked her for her kind consideration and told her my integrity is not for sale.

I walked out without a source of income, uncertain of how I would pay the bills and support my family, but I held my head high. My integrity was intact.

For the next few days, I thoroughly enjoyed the process of detoxing from the organization I left behind. My shoulders felt lighter and my heart filled with the excitement for new possibilities. However, as the days turned into weeks, I began to experience the familiar whispers and images. My old foe was back inside my head, raising the volume on what had been lowered for so long. This time, my inner voice of doom used a new weapon. It started with a financial hypothesis.

"For the past 15 years, you barely brought home the bacon. Your family had to sacrifice so that you could selfishly pursue your dreams. You finally land a job so you can provide for them, only to quit after a year? You weak, whiny, and selfish P.O.S. You know... you are worth more dead than alive, aren't you? Alexis has a couple of life insurance policies on you. Compared to the bacon bits you have been bringing home, the amount of money your family would collect from your life insurance would be so much more. Your children are young enough to forget about you. Alexis is young enough to find another husband. In fact, she could get a far better husband who could properly provide and support your family. You clearly can't do it for them, so let someone else do it for them. Your family deserves better. They deserve someone better than you."

Flashes of spreadsheets filled my mind. While I couldn't make out the details, I recognized the formatting. It was identical to the financial modeling template I used to for my businesses and clients. The message was loud and clear. I was financially worth more dead to my family than alive. I rebutted my inner voice of doom, "But the life insurance policy does not cover suicide, you idiot. Go back to your corner and keep your mouth shut!"

I thought I owned the voice again.

My 48th birthday had a foggy and snowy start. As I was getting my son ready for school, I heard the voice return. I kept myself distracted as I helped Mateo get ready for school. I had been struggling with what the voice had said a few days ago; it felt like it was slowly chipping away at my rational mind. After dropping Mateo off at school, I decided to drive up to one of my favorite spots and clear my head. The drive up to Evergreen Lake through the sleepy towns of Morrison and Idledale was as pleasant as always. As I sat with a hot cup of coffee overlooking the lake, that inner voice started to speak again. It came back with a proposal to mitigate the critical flaw I had found in its financial hypothesis.

"You have a medical history of blacking out, so all you have to do is noticeably swerve a few times on the road and then drive your car into the side of a mountain or off into a valley. Everyone would think you blacked out again, including the life insurance companies. You will be covered!"

My inner voice of doom was trying to logically reason with me. It built a financial model to prove that I am worth more dead than alive. It assessed the known risks and developed a mitigation plan. These are two of my critical skills as an entrepreneur and strategist. I realized that while this inner voice may not be my own, it has access to everything I am thinking and feeling, including my strengths and skills. It truly was an internal battle. It felt like I was going to implode. I hurriedly finished my coffee and decided to go back home, not realizing the biggest battle was still to come.

I thought it would be safer to drive back on the highway than on the windy road I took to get up to Evergreen Lake. I thought all the turns on its tiny two lanes through Idledale and Morrison would only provide more ammunition for the inner voice of doom. When I got to I-70, the fog was heavy above the wet pavement. As soon as I merged onto the highway, the voice kicked into high gear.

"Here we go. Now is the perfect time. There is a cliff coming up ahead to the right. Swerve now, speed up, and drive off that edge. Help your family now.

Do the right thing!"

I fought the voice harder than ever before and locked both hands onto the steering wheel during the entire 15-minute drive, which felt like an eternity. My family's faces flashed in my mind, including my mom's. I was reminded of the Korean saying, "The most terrible tragedy that can happen to a person is burying his or her own child." I wasn't about to do that to my mother.

"Fuck you, voice," I screamed inside my head. "There will be no implosion. I am not checking out today".

I broke down that night and told Alexis about my inner voice of doom and what had happened. I didn't want to burden her any more than I already had, but I wanted her to know that my mood, attitude, and behavior had nothing to do with her or our children. The shitstorm was all inside my head.

In the following days and weeks, I worked on my own financial modeling to fight against my inner voice of doom. I had to fight fire with fire. If it is using my own strengths to attack me, I would use the same strengths to go on offense and prove it wrong. I could also use my other strengths, grit and hustle, to deliver a better financial return and take better care of my family. I wanted to prove that I am worth more alive than dead. Just like I did on the return trip to Seattle, I wanted to prove the voice wrong.

I realize not everyone may be able to identify with harmful inner voices, thoughts, or images. If you have never suffered from these elements within yourself, you are blessed. Please continue living your life, and do not overanalyze your inner dialogue. If you have experienced these elements before, I invite you to identify, acknowledge, and find a healthy way to manage them. They are not you, but they are a part of you that you have to deal with. If you do not find a way to manage them effectively, they will run amuck and wreak havoc on your life. Please note that not all inner voices, thoughts, and images are harmful. There are positive inner voices of love, care, inspiration, wisdom, and patience. It is important to identify and acknowledge them all. The first step is to pay close attention to what you are hearing, feeling, and seeing in your mind. Recognition and acknowledgment are the first steps. Once you have taken stock, figure out where they might have come from. As my voice of doom is a collective voice, you may have a similar coalition of voices representing a certain character trait or period of time from your life. Name those voices. Do they mimic actual people in your life? Or do they simply represent emotions or archetypes? Use names, nouns, or adjectives to precisely identify them. You have to acknowledge the cast members inside your head before you can effectively direct them in your life's story.

> *Please use the following worksheet in* The Life ROI Workbook *to complete this step of the framework:* RESEARCH | Inner Voices Worksheet

Life ROI Framework: Analysis

Value Analysis

In the Research phase, we solicited help from our personal brand ambassadors to gain a better understanding of ourselves and our value. Now that we have gathered their insightful and honest feedback, we will dive into analyzing the valuable data.

The first step is Value Analysis. The following questions are designed to gauge how your personal brand ambassadors perceive your personal brand values. Answers from the following questions will be used to shape your analysis:

- Question 1: What do you think are my top strengths? Please list up to three strengths.
- Question 2: What areas can I improve in? Please list up to three areas of development.
- Question 7: Which popular consumer brand do you associate with me (e.g. Nike, Apple, Gatorade, Toyota, etc.)? Which of the brand's attributes remind you of me?
- Question 8: How would you describe me in one sentence to someone who does not know me?

- Question 9: What ONE word would you choose to describe me? Why have you chosen this word for me?

Using the Value Analysis worksheet, please list all of the attributes that your personal brand ambassadors identified in the following categories:

- Strengths
- Weakness
- Brand attribute associations
- One-sentence tagline
- One-word descriptor

Once you have written them down, please use the columns on the right-side of the worksheet to assess whether each attribute would be considered functional or emotional in nature based on the context of the answers they were given in. Please note that some attributes may be considered both functional and emotional, in which case please check both columns. When completed, please add up the checkmarks in each column to see whether you have more functional or emotional attributes. There is no such thing as the perfect or ideal balance between the two categories of attributes. You must sit with the total sum of each category and any difference between them for a while. If you receive more functional attributes, it means that your personal brand ambassadors perceive you to be more of a functional person. They identify you as a person more closely defined by what you do and how you do it. If you receive more emotional attributes, it means that your personal brand ambassadors identify you as a person more closely defined by who you are and how you make them feel. If you have ever taken a personality test, regardless of the methodology, you have an idea of where you fall on this scale between functional and emotional. However, how you think of yourself may be different than how your personal brand ambassadors perceive you to be. Here are some key questions to ask yourself in this analysis:

- Are you satisfied with the balance between your functional and emotional attributes?
- Are you surprised by any of the responses? If so, why?
- Are your personal brand ambassadors perceiving you the way you want them to?
- Are their perceptions aligned with how you present yourself and behave?
- Are there any gaps between your own answers and theirs?
- What do you think created this gap?

> *Please use the following worksheet in The Life ROI Workbook to complete this step of the framework:* ANALYSIS | Value Analysis Worksheet

SWOT Analysis

SWOT analysis is a cornerstone of any market, industry, or competitive analysis. Conducting a thorough assessment of internal and external strengths, weaknesses, opportunities, and threats can ensure successful outcomes at a higher probability. However, conducting a SWOT analysis on ourselves and our personal brand is not a common practice. However, if it can provide meaningful and effective value to businesses, I believe it can provide the same to us as well.

This analysis utilizes the answers you received from the following questions in the 360 research questionnaire:

- Question 1: What do you think are my top strengths? Please list up to three strengths.
- Question 2: In what areas can I improve? Please list up to three areas of development.

Here is how we conduct SWOT analysis differently for personal branding. It is not enough to simply identify our strengths. We have to do some further investigation to understand how they became our strengths. Did we inherit them from winning the genetic lottery? Or did we work our butts off to gain them on our own? For example, if height is one of your strengths, which allowed you to join the varsity basketball team as a freshman and you became one of the highest-performing players because dunking came so naturally to you, this strength is not really yours to own. You simply cashed in on an inherited trait. However, if you worked on your three-point shot by showing up early to practice every day and staying late every evening, and you became the highest-scoring player on the team, then that strength is all yours. You paid your dues for it.

ORIGIN   **STRENGTH**   **OPPORTUNITY**

Becoming the highest-scoring player was an opportunity you took because you properly leveraged your earned strength. I believe the only way to gain authentic confidence is to acknowledge what you have earned and how hard you worked for it. Taking note of all the sacrifice, sweat, blood, and tears you poured into your accomplishments is the only way to own your strength. This way, you know you can do it again. The environment, audience, context, and opportunity might differ, but your ability to grit and hustle remain the same. It is all yours. You can turn it on and face any challenge with confidence because of your personal history. No one can take that away from you.

Attributes of weakness need to be analyzed differently but with the same intention as strengths. In order to truly acknowledge these attributes as our weaknesses, we must begin by finding out their causes. Are some of these weakness attributes associated with inner voices? Through nature, did we inherit these weaknesses? Or through our own experience, did we develop them and use them as automatic responses to protect ourselves? What caused your weaknesses to form, and how have your life experiences and relationships affected them?

CAUSE   **WEAKNESS**   **THREAT**

For example, say you grew up in a volatile environment that continually activated your fight-or-flight response. You have been able to identify certain words, facial expressions, and behaviors as triggers throughout your life. You have survived multiple threats, both perceived and actual, and have come to rely on these triggers for self-preservation. You are now an adult, working in a professional environment and seeking a meaningful long-term relationship with a significant other. Throughout the week, you feel triggered by colleagues and the person you are dating. They are not aware of what happened. Most of these triggers were accidental and weren't delivered with malicious intent. However, these triggers and your subsequent reactions are deeply wired inside of you. You automatically respond to these triggers. In some occasions, you immediately leave because you want to protect yourself. In other occasions, you dig your heels in and go on offense to protect yourself. You never question whether your reactions are justified because they have served you so long. What you may not realize is that while your triggers and automatic reactions may have served you well in the past, they may no longer serve you in new environments and with different people. We have legitimate reasons to carry around baggage from traumatic and harmful experiences, but we are not entitled to dump that baggage onto someone else. If we continue to automatically respond to triggers without analyzing the situation and the people involved, these triggered reactions become our weaknesses. These weaknesses can then lead you to hurt or threaten to hurt innocent people and sabotage your own relationships.

Each component in SWOT analysis is closely interconnected with each other and cannot be isolated. Opportunities can only be realized and accomplished when they are meaningfully aligned with your strengths. While we can identify threats, we do not have 100% control over the external factors that cause them. What we do have control over is how our weaknesses may instigate self-sabotaging threats against ourselves. We can identify the original cause for these weaknesses and manage them effectively in order to reduce their frequency of occurrence.

> Please use the following worksheet in The Life ROI Workbook to complete this step of the framework: **ANALYSIS | SWOT Analysis Worksheet**

Balance Sheet Analysis

A balance sheet is a financial analysis of an organization used to show its financial health. The total sum of assets and liabilities accounts for all that the organization owns and owes. The information provided is binary in nature. For personal branding, the balance sheet is dynamic. While it should have a similar structure, the assets column is for your strength attributes and the liabilities column is for your weakness attributes. However, your strengths are not always your assets and your weaknesses are not always your liabilities. Depending on the context and environment, attributes are dynamic and can change classifications. In any given situation, your strengths can become your weaknesses and vice versa.

The following questions from the 360 research will be used for this analysis:

- Question 1: What do you think are my top strengths? Please list up to three strengths.
- Question 2: In what areas can I improve? Please list up to three areas of development.
- Question 5: In which environment or situation do you think I am at my best? Please describe your observation or experience.

Here is an example. One of the most popular one-word descriptors my students and clients have received from their personal brand ambassadors is "driven." It also happens to be the word my wife chose for my one-word descriptor. I thought "driven" justifiably belongs to the assets column as a strength attribute for most people, especially for entrepreneurs. Let me demonstrate how a strength attribute like "driven" gets analyzed in the balance sheet. In a professional environment where I am accountable for my investors, clients, colleagues, and staff, being driven is a strength which enables me to be effective. In this context, "driven" is a strength attribute filed under the assets column. However, being driven is an absolute weakness in my personal life. My family does not benefit from a father and husband who was so driven that he is never home. Earlier in my life, I worked around the clock and spent one half-day at home a week when I first started my business. When I was home, I was exhausted so I would typically sleep or interact with my family in a vegetative state of mind. My family did not want me to be this driven, they wanted me to be present in their lives. They needed me to be aware, engaged, available, and loving at home. In the context of a personal environment and my family, "driven" is a weakness attribute filed under the liabilities column on my balance sheet. I also came to find out that Alexis began associating my workaholic behavior with the negative connotations of being driven: being stubborn, rigid, and bullheaded. None of these definitions represent the character traits I would want my wife to associate me with nor how I want to be remembered by my children when I am gone.

The balance sheet can also account for simpler attributes like humor. Whether you are funny or not is not up to you to determine. It is up to those who interact with you and have experienced your sense of humor. Certain attributes can be categorized as either assets or liabilities depending on who is making the call. Humor can absolutely act as a strength in certain environments and with certain people, but it can also have the opposite effect in different circumstances.

Sometimes, you may find that a weakness attribute that typically belongs in the liabilities column can also serve as a strength attribute in certain environments and with certain people. The attribute of being "laid back" can be a huge liability in a fast-paced professional environment. However, in a therapeutic and people-focused environment, "laid back" can be synonymous with "patience" and serve as an asset.

I have seen emotionally intelligent leaders who practice vulnerability and empathy be labeled as weak. How could this be possible when vulnerability and empathy are considered to be two of the most critical leadership qualities in most contemporary leadership books? If the organization is in a production-focused industry and success is determined by volume and price. It is possible that the culture does not value the mental, emotional, or physical well-being of its people, and emotional intelligence may not be appreciated much. The opposite scenario may also be possible. If the organization is in the people business, leveraging relationship and trust to deliver quality outcomes, the culture may not value volume-driven, speed focused, and strictly functional mindset. In this culture, implementation focused leader who prioritizes tactics over people may not be effective or appreciated. Understanding your environments and people in it will allow you to effectively leverage your strengths to pursue meaningful opportunities. Reflect on the answers you received for Question 5 and see if there are meaningful correlations between your strengths and when you were at your best. Here are some questions you should ask yourself:

- When you were observed to be at your best, was it because you were effectively leveraging your assets?
- More than correlation, can you establish a direct causation between your assets and when you were at your best?
- Were you ever at your best when you weren't leveraging your assets? If so, what do you think made that possible?

> *Please use the following worksheet in The Life ROI Workbook to complete this step of the framework:* ANALYSIS | Balance Sheet Worksheet

Environment & Audience Analysis

Analyzing your environment and audience will help you identify where your happiness and stress exist and who or what created them. A perceptual mapping exercise is included in this section to help you see your life from an elevated perspective. This elevated view is similar to an analysts' view during a football game. The players see each play from the ground level on the field, but their vision is limited to what they can see out of their helmets and from their individual positions. Coaches on the sidelines have a broader vision and a different perspective but are still on the ground level. Analysts have a comprehensive view of the entire field from an elevated position that allows them to strategically analyze what is happening. Their perspective allows them to see how both teams are playing, where opportunities and threat may exist, and how each play is planned out throughout the game. Gaining an analysts' perspective on your life will help you make informed and dynamic decisions to win the game.

Answers from the following questions are used in this analysis:

- Question 3: When was the last time you saw me at my happiest? Please describe the occasion and the circumstances.
- Question 4: When was the last time you saw me stressed out? Please describe the occasion and the circumstances.
- Question 5: In which environment or situation do you think I am at my best? Please describe your observation or experience.
- Question 6: If you were to make a highlight reel on my life, what one scene would you make sure to include?
- Question 10: Is there anything you would like to see me add to my life that may be currently missing?

From the answers you received from your personal brand ambassadors, you will be able to see where you were, who you were with, what took place, and the context in which they observed you experience happiness or stress. The answers to Question 5 and 6 will also reveal the details that surround the most important moments of your life and what environments allow you to thrive. You must reflect on and compare these details against your own memory. As I stated earlier, because it is impossible for us to see ourselves from all angles, Question 10 can shed light on what we may be missing or confirm our aspirations. Do your personal brand ambassadors reveal gaps in your professional or personal life? For most single people, you will likely receive feedback about dating or marriage from your family. For those who are married but do not have any children, you will likely receive feedback about starting a family. If you are a busy professional who is "driven," you may receive feedback about self-care, rest, and relaxation.

Based on the results of this analysis and perceptual map, here are questions you should ask yourself:

- Does your perceptual map accurately represent what causes your happiness and stress and where it happens?

- Does your memory align with how your personal brand ambassadors observed those circumstances of happiness, stress? Does your self-perception align with that they chose for your best environment and the scene for your highlight reel?

- Is there any unexpected feedback on these circumstances? If so, why were you surprised by their feedback? Is there any merit to the difference between what you expected and what they said?

- Is there anything you can do to change the environment and people causing you stress in your professional and personal life?

- Do you recognize any correlations between your strengths, the people, the culture, and the environment where you were at your best?

- If you were able to establish any correlations in Question 5, can you intentionally and repeatedly recreate or find those circumstances?

- Do you agree with the responses to Question 10? If not, how would you reconcile your disagreement?

> *Please use the following worksheet in* The Life ROI Workbook *to complete this step of the framework:* **ANALYSIS | Environment & Audience Analysis Worksheet**

Life ROI Framework: Strategy

Strategic Alignment

In an earlier chapter, I shared how I thought that the way we have been taught to define success in our society and culture is flawed. I expressed how critical it is for each individual to define their own success and own their journey. You have just completed the exhaustive process of gathering comprehensive data on your personal brand and analyzing it. Congratulations, and thank you for getting through this process as I know it can be quite difficult for many people.

The results from your analyses should paint a clear and comprehensive picture of your personal brand: your core values, your loves and fears, your strengths and weaknesses, your assets and liabilities, and how environments and people impact your happiness and stress. This 360 research and analyses should have also distinguished the intrinsic and extrinsic motivations, loves, fears, and scorecards in your mind and heart. As members of a family, company, community, and society, we have to acknowledge the importance of extrinsic scorecards and demands. It would be nearly impossible for most of us to completely cut off extrinsic elements and motivations and live a life as a hermit. The goal is to establish a healthy harmony between intrinsic and extrinsic demands. I am purposeful in using the term "harmony" here rather than "balance." Balance can automatically create a mental image of a perfectly level scale with both ends in line. The mere thought of achieving this perfect balance stresses me out. Also, the common mental image associated with balance implies that it is binary. There are typically only two components involved in the act of balancing. For most of us, life is not so simple. Typically, we all are faced with decisions that have multiple factors, options, and outcomes. Since the days of kindergarten, life choices have rarely been as simple as yes or no. To me, harmony communicates complexity, where many things coexist. Also, I am not disillusioned to expect a perfect picture of infinite happiness with unicorns and rainbows.

Let's go to the trusty Dictionary.com again:

Harmony [hahr-muh-nee] [2]

- agreement; accord; harmonious relations.
- a consistent, orderly, or pleasing arrangement of parts; congruity.
- Music.
  - any simultaneous combination of tones.
  - the simultaneous combination of tones, especially when blended into chords pleasing to the ear; chordal structure, as distinguished from melody and rhythm.
  - the science of the structure, relations, and practical combination of chords.
- ORIGIN OF HARMONY
  1350–1400); Middle English armonye < Middle French < Latin harmonia < Greek harmonía joint, framework, agreement, harmony, akin to hárma chariot, harmós joint, araáriskein to join together

---

[2] "Harmony," Dictionary.com, accessed May 10, 2020,
https://www.dictionary.com/browse/harmony.

As included in the Greek root of armonía, harmony is a framework, something that is foundational but also flexible. It is solid enough to build upon, but it also provides openings to revise and refine. It is an ongoing and continual work-in-progress, unlike balance where you work your butt off to achieve it and then have to continuously work to maintain it.

Also, the way harmony is defined in music accurately represents what we are striving for in life. "Harmony is the blending of simultaneous sounds of different pitch or quality, making chords." Let's replace some of those words in the definition with words that resonate and apply directly to life:

- Replace "sounds" with "people, demand, and responsibility."
- Replace "different pitch or quality" with "time, attention, and commitment."
- Replace "making chords" with "living with intentions."

When we embrace harmony as a goal in our daily lives, the following acknowledgments and realizations will guide us:

- Life is complex, but it doesn't have to be complicated if we honestly embrace the fact that life is not meant to be simple.
- It's impossible to give 100% of our attention to all of the people in our lives.
- It's impossible to give 100% of our attention to all of the things we have to do.
- There is no such thing as "perfect" in life.
- It is meant to be messy sometimes.
- We are not going to win every time.
- We are not going to lose every time.
- We fail, but we learn so we can pivot and refine.
- We only have access to 24 hours a day. The next 24 is not guaranteed.

- We may not get everything we need to or want to get done in a day.

- Make sure there is intention behind everything that we do in our day.

- Do not put off the important things until tomorrow, as we are promised only today.

- Make sure we wisely and purposefully invest our time to the people and actions that matter the most to us.

I came across a Japanese diagram called Ikigai, which represents a sense of having meaning, direction, and purpose in life. It really resonated with me on so many levels. Plus, consultants are suckers for good Venn diagrams. While the Ikigai diagram was thorough and well designed, I needed one that better fit with my journey and my current reality. So, I made a simpler version by adapting the most relevant and meaningful components. I have been using this diagram to strategically align the major aspects of my life and create strategic direction for what I want to strive for.

Strategic Alignment

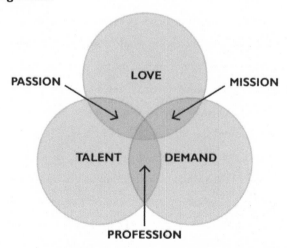

LOVE

Let's start with the love component. For the purposes of this diagram, the definition of love is the old-school, genuine, deep, and nuclear level of love. It is the truest love, not the type you post for on social media or how you "love" a venti mocha latte with almond milk, light foam, and a sprinkle of cinnamon. I mean what you really love. Someone or something you would sacrifice everything to protect. Someone or something you would be driven to extreme anger to protect. I believe what you really love can drive you to eruptive anger. The deeper you love someone or something, the more severe your efforts will be to protect them or it. You may not react with anger when something interrupts what you like; you may become frustrated but not angry. This is because you do not have the same level of emotional investment in something you merely like. This is a law of human nature.

In my case, I love children — not just my own, but all children. Obviously, I would do anything to protect my children as a father. Like all parents, the thought of my children getting hurt breaks my heart and the thought of someone intentionally hurting my children enrages me. For example, on a rainy morning in September 2015, I had just dropped my daughter off at school and I was driving to work when I heard about a 3-year-old Syrian boy on NPR. My heart sank as I heard how this little boy's body washed up on the shore of Turkey. NPR moved on to other news story, but I was stuck visualizing this boy's body on the beach and processing what could have led to his untimely and tragic end. As I sat at a red light, I picked up my phone to distract myself from these morbid thoughts. I decided to check my Facebook feed. The first post I saw was a picture of the same Syrian boy's lifeless body on the beach with Turkish soldiers standing around him. He was tiny. He didn't look all that different from how I saw my 4-year-old son sleeping in his bed that morning when I left the house. That's when overwhelming anger rushed in. The light was no longer the only thing red in my eyes. I wanted to go after every single adult who created such circumstances that forced this little boy's parents to make the most difficult decision of their lives. I couldn't imagine having to flee with my family into uncertainty because it was simply the only option for survival. My grandparents on both sides had to make a similar difficult decision when the

Korean War broke out in 1950. What would I do? I would do the same. I would choose uncertainty over the certain death of my family, no matter how scary it may be. I was furious. I would have lashed out in violence if the people responsible for this boy's death were in front of me in that moment. I had to turn my car around and head home. I couldn't function mentally or emotionally. I had to go home, hug my 4-year-old boy, love him, and reflect on my blessings. I remember how I struggled with a blurry vision on my drive home, and it was not from the rain.

Reflecting on that morning in 2015 helped me understand how I have always loved children, long before I was blessed with my own. I love children because they are so pure, innocent, and true. We are all born as perfect human beings. But slowly and surely, we lose our perfection through all the pollution and corruption in this world. My love for children has been there for the longest time, but I had noticed it only through fun and positive interactions with children. That changed on that morning in 2015. The Syrian boy's name was Aylan. Aylan's tragic death was the first time my love for children was tested and led to my pendulum swinging to the other side. I believe our true love is tested when it is violated. Therefore, I think we are able to identify and validate our love by revisiting the moments in our lives when we experienced extreme levels of anger because whom and what we loved were violated.

The following questions may be simple to answer for some people, but for others, it may present some challenges. Start by thinking of all the people and things that you think you love in your life and ask yourself, "Do I love this person/thing because I think I have to? Or is it because I choose to?" When you have successfully answered this question, please proceed with the following questions, but include only those people and things that you willingly choose to love.

- Who do you love?

147

- What do you love?
- What do you love to do?
- Why do you love who you love?
- Why do you love what you love?
- Why do you love what you love to do?

TALENT

The definition of talent for our purposes is divided into two parts: 1) the gift you were awarded from winning the genetic lottery and 2) hard-earned rewards that you worked your butt off to attain. Regardless of how you acquired your talents, identify what you are or have been good at in life. Then, validate them to ensure that you are indeed good at them. Are you really good at what you claim to be good at? Is it true? Has it been confirmed or recognized by others? Have others offered to compensate you because your talents provided benefits to them? Praises from your grandparents or parents do not count. You may go back to the results from the SWOT, Balance Sheet, and Environment & Audience analyses to identify your true and validated talents.

DEMAND

This is a simpler concept. This is what the world requires of you at all levels. At the micro-level, demands are made by your family, friends, and company. At the macro-level, demands are made by your community, country, and the world. Some of these demands are explicitly stated and known. However, some of these demands are implicit and not so apparent. These implicit demands may exist among those who are really close to you at the micro-level or those who lack the resources and suffer from inequity at the macro-level. Keep your eyes and ears open. Be curious and ask questions.

LOVE + TALENT = PASSION

There are plenty of ways to define passion because the term is often so subjective and personal. As long as the definition is relevant, meaningful, and practical to your life, any definition is fair game. Here is my perspective on and definition for passion:

Passion can be found in the activities that engage you and cause you to simply lose track of time. It can be whatever makes the hours fly by for you. Very few of us sit down to work at our offices and look up to see that eight hours somehow flew by. When you love what you are doing, time is easy to lose track of because you want it to go on forever. If anything, you want time to stop so you don't have to quit what you are doing. The motivation to engage in these activities is intrinsic. You do not need anyone to remind or force you to keep going. Practicing these activities often invokes raw emotions of joy, fulfillment, and happiness. When violated or taken away, the pendulum will swing and cause you to experience raw emotions of anger. You often leverage your talents during these activities, and you just as often gain confidence from continued practice. These activities generate endorphins, or the feel-good chemicals in your brain, that further motivate you to keep practicing and developing your talents. It is a healthy, cyclical process of love, talent, practice, and confidence that feed into one another. This is the practice of passion.

TALENT + DEMAND = PROFESSION

Talent in the absence of demand will not amount to a profession. You may be great at something that is not in demand, like underwater basket weaving. That's perfectly ok. This just means that it should be a hobby instead of a profession. When your talent aligns with something that is in demand, and others are willing to compensate you for it, then you have a profession. This should be mutually beneficial in nature, with the outcome of your talents being exchanged for a fair and market-driven compensation. Of course, there are layers of complexity involved in defining mutual and fair benefits. If you do not feel that you are being fairly compensated for your talent, you must determine what the contributing factors, both intrinsic and extrinsic are. Then you should develop a tactical plan to address and mitigate these intrinsic and extrinsic factors appropriately. Please keep in mind that everyone has their own risk tolerance, as well as unique circumstances and challenges, so the final decision is up to the individual. I believe that when we reach our maximum capacity for tolerating unfair compensation, we either accept the disparity or we change our course for the unknown to find a better option worth pursuing.

DEMAND + LOVE = MISSION

Mission is not financially motivated. If you're only after financial reward, please return to the profession section above. When you find a community that has demand for what you love, you can practice your mission with a sense of purpose and commitment. The decisions and activities associated with your mission are not about you but those you serve. In Colorado, there are over 20,000 registered nonprofits. I believe every single one of those nonprofits strive to serve their communities to the best of their abilities with what they have. The larger nonprofits are much more visible in our society at large due to their access to resources. They simply have more resources compared to the smaller nonprofits operating out of their founder's basement or garage. Regardless of their sizes, all nonprofits struggle with common challenges. Most people think of financial donations and fundraising when it comes to supporting nonprofit work. In fact, I've been conducting an informal survey with my undergraduate and graduate students, and while it does not meet any legitimate research requirements, I would like to share my findings with you anyway. In every class, I ask how many students volunteer on a regular basis. Usually 80% of undergraduate students raise their hand, compared to less than 20% of graduate students. I have heard many justifications from my graduate students, such as:

"I donate, so I don't think I need to volunteer."

"I am so busy with work, marriage, and kids. I just can't find the time."

"I have been meaning to, but I have a hard time finding the right organization to volunteer for."

"I want to, but I don't know where to start."

These are all legitimate reasons. As we grow older, our responsibilities grow more and more. It becomes increasingly difficult to juggle and prioritize all that we have to do. However, if you value and enjoy helping or serving others, you may want to make it a priority in your life. If serving or helping others is one of your true loves, just remember that you will experience stress if you don't get to practice them.

For parents who want to raise productive, empathetic, and compassionate future members of society, walking the talk is much more effective than just talking the talk. I encourage you to consider modeling what compassion and generosity in practice looks, feels, and sounds like for your children. For the professionals who think you can't afford to help because the only way to help is through financial donations, may I disrupt that paradigm slightly? Smaller nonprofits desperately need the skills and talents of professionals like yourself. What you get paid to do from 9 to 5 every day is exactly what these organizations need help with: accounting, marketing, writing, social media, IT, management, operations, etc. Small nonprofits need financial donations, but they also desperately need people's skills, talents, and time to run and grow their operations successfully. Your contribution of time and expertise can help them fill a void in their organization. I have attended various nonprofit galas over the years. These events serve as fantastic platforms to showcase their impact, build awareness, deepen their community relationships, and raise the funding they need to continue their meaningful work. You will meet good people at these events, good people who purchased tickets, took the time to show up, and even bid on auction items to increase their level of support. There is another group of good people behind the scenes, but you can only meet them if you volunteer. These good people give not only their money, but they also give their most valuable asset: time. They commit to give their time for the benefit of others. Often, volunteer work is not glamorous and does not involve tuxedos and fancy dresses, fun photo walls, and schwag bags. These good people show up and do what they can to benefit others, and yet they always say that they gained more from the experience than what they gave. I can concur from my own experience. Receiving gifts is fun, but giving gifts is exhilaratingly inspirational. Please continue to support galas and fundraising events, but also consider sharing your most valuable asset and volunteer. Your return on investment from volunteering is guaranteed to yield a high return.

It is my sincere hope that when you have gone through this Strategic Alignment diagram, you can better understand which sections you currently thrive in and which sections you may want to invest more time, intention, and focus. I have had some students and clients conclude that the mission section should be put on hold until they have more disposable income and time. Some expressed the need to push out the mission section altogether until they retire. Some of you reading this book right now may share this opinion as well. I respect their perspective and yours. However, I invite you to consider the following before putting mission on hold:

- As I discussed earlier, there is no guarantee that you will reach the golden years of retirement. We save and hope for the best, but it is not promised to us, just as tomorrow is not promised.
- If serving and helping others is really important to you and you experience joy, fulfillment, and happiness while doing so, why would you put it off? Wouldn't you want to intentionally invest your time to experience joy, fulfillment, and happiness sooner and more frequently?

When we are intentionally working on all sections of this Strategic Alignment diagram, we are diligently working to increase our Life ROI. By prioritizing your actions in alignment with your personal brand values, you can live your life with a higher yield in satisfaction, fulfillment, and happiness.

> *Please use the following worksheet in The Life ROI Workbook to complete this step of*

Strategic Design

Many top athletes practice image training to elevate their performance. They visualize their actions in their minds, carefully going through each play, and picturing themselves holding up the trophy or a medal in triumph.

I believe the ability to visualize what we want to achieve can help focus and inspire us forward with a higher probability of succeeding. Most of us fear the dark because we cannot see what is hiding in the shadows. When we shed light on dark spaces and realize that it was just a tiny mouse making the noise which initially sounded like a monster's growl, we are no longer scared. I think the opposite happens when we can see what we want. We get excited, inspired, and energized. Then we become more focused, purposeful, and intentional.

I invite you to visualize THAT DAY, which represents the first day of the rest of your life when you no longer have to do anything that is not aligned with your values. On THAT DAY and beyond, you get to do everything you want to do and not a single thing else. This is not retirement, especially not in the way it is conventionally defined. On THAT DAY, your schedule is filled with intentional, purposeful, and meaningful activities that you desire. You get to visualize THAT DAY however you imagine, based on your own terms. It's all yours!

There are two methods to this exercise. You can choose to do one or both:

A. First, find a quiet and private space or somewhere you can put headphones on and listen to music that puts you in a peaceful state of mind. Then, close your eyes and picture THAT DAY, starting with when you wake up in the morning. Visualize your entire day, who you interact with, what activities you do, and what environments you are in. Once you have gone through the entire day, open your eyes and document what you visualized on the Strategic Design worksheet. Include as much detail as possible.

B. If you are not a visual person, you can jump straight to filling out the worksheet. Utilize the results from the questionnaire, balance sheet, and environment and audience analysis to help you design THAT DAY.

Regardless of which method you use, please be as descriptive as possible and include everything, from the moment you wake up till the moment you go to sleep and EVERYTHING in between. Remember THAT DAY's schedule is only filled with what you want to do and not what you have to do. The more details you can visualize and document, the more real THAT DAY becomes, and the more ownership you will have. This will make it more feasible, and you will feel more motivated.

Here are some questions to guide you as you design THAT DAY:

- What time are you waking up?
- Who are you waking up next to? Or are you alone?
- What is the first thing you do after waking up?
- What are you eating for breakfast? Why are you eating this for breakfast?
- What are you doing after breakfast?
- Are you going to work?
- What are you doing for work?
- Why are you still working?
- Who do you work with?
- Why do you choose to work with these people?
- What are you having for lunch? Why are you having this for lunch?

- Are you eating alone or with other people?
- Why are you choosing to have lunch with these people?
- What are you doing in the afternoon?
- What time will you get home?
- Is there someone waiting for you at home?
- Why is this person waiting for you?
- What are you having for dinner? Why are you having this for dinner?
- Are you cooking dinner or is someone else?
- What are you doing after dinner?
- Why are you choosing to do this after dinner?
- What time are you going to sleep?
- Why are you choosing to go to sleep at this time?

One of the most powerful impacts of this visualization exercise is the practical comparison between THAT DAY and your typical day now. Once you have designed your schedule of activities for THAT DAY, I encourage you to choose one activity and schedule it on your calendar next week or month. Do your best to commit to it, as work and family obligations will try to either force you or guilt you into canceling. Protect it. Follow through and try living out a small portion of THAT DAY in your normal schedule. Once you have completed that activity, reflect on the experience and ask yourself whether it was as great as you had imagined. If it was, put it on your calendar again. Then, plan a second activity, a third, a fourth, and so on. Follow this rinse-and-repeat regimen and live THAT DAY in smaller portions throughout your life. Once you get the taste of THAT DAY, you will no longer need any self-help books, motivational speakers, or daily inspirational quotes to motivate you. The intrinsic motivation from experiencing the authentic alignment of your values, love, and passion will drive you to live your life with confidence and intention. You will own your way, journey, and life.

In one of my Life ROI seminars, I had a student who spent less than 20 minutes to document his version of THAT DAY, while the majority of his cohort struggled for hours. Some may assume that he must have hastily completed the worksheet without much commitment or thought. In truth, that had nothing to do with why he spent such a short amount of time completing the worksheet. His commitment was far deeper because he had been visualizing THAT DAY long before the seminar, so it was easier for him. When he read his THAT DAY aloud during the seminar, the entire cohort was genuinely moved and enthusiastically inspired to work on their own THAT DAY.

Here is Tom Nazzaro's THAT DAY:

Weekdays

Morning:
- We both have dual citizenship and are living in Italy.
- Wake up at our house/apartment in Italy around 4:30 a.m. and go out to the vineyard to pick some grapes and figs from the tree. Go back to the house and put on some music and start a pot of coffee.
- Go into the bedroom and say to Becky, "Buongiorno. Come stai?"
- Becky wakes up and comes to the kitchen, and we have breakfast together and discuss what we will do today. After breakfast, Becky gets ready and we go to town.

Afternoon:
- We ride our bikes into the small Italian village and visit the open markets to look for dinner. On the way, we stop and have an espresso at a small bar (that's what the Italians call a coffee shop) and share a pastry. When we get to the market, the vendors have a wide variety of freshly pick vegetables available for sale. We purchase some fresh tomatoes, spinach, garlic, melons, and whatever else looks good. We pick up a bottle of extra virgin olive oil from the region.
- Becky and I go to the bakery to buy a freshly baked loaf of Italian bread

and some mixed olives to complete the dinner. As we are walking through town, we go to our favorite wine store and choose a bottle of Amarone. Becky decides that we need something sweet for after the meal, so we decide to look at the fresh pastries and buy a variety to try.

- It's about time to get back home but we need a few more additions for tonight's meal. We all go to the butcher shop and buy some prosciutto and fresh pasta. We put the groceries and wine into baskets on our bikes and return home.

Evening:

- Becky decides that it is time to some pre-dinner cocktails, so we both have Campari and sodas. Then I start to prepare dinner. Becky wants to listen to some country music, but it's really hard to find that music in Italy, so we decide to listen to some music from Frank and Dino's instead.

- Becky sets the table. I open our bottle of Amarone and pour us both a glass to enjoy before we eat. We sit at the table and enjoy some fresh pasta and tomato sauce made from our purchases in town. Dinner is great, and I decide to have some coffee while Becky continues to enjoy the wine.

- We open the box of pastries, drink our drinks, and listen to great music. It is a great night at home.

Weekends

Morning:

- Becky and I wake up early at 4:30 a.m.
- Today, Sergio, Lizzie, and Corina are coming to visit with their new baby.
- Becky makes sure everyone had clean sheets and tells me to clean the kitchen and living room because she wants the house to look great for everyone.

- I take a quick trip into town to make sure we have enough wine and food for everyone.

Afternoon:

- Becky and I go to the airport to pick up our guests. Becky welcomes the baby, who greets Becky in Italian. This makes her very happy.
- We go back to our house and everyone goes to their rooms to unpack. We open up a bottle of Prosecco and toast the fact that we are all together in Italy.
- Sergio decides that he wants to buy a bottle of Brunello di Montalcino for dinner.

Evening:

- We all get dressed, have some appetizers, and open the bottle of wine that Sergio bought. Becky and I had already made a reservation at our favorite restaurant in town, and we can't wait to take everyone there.
- We get to the restaurant and the owner, who we personally know, greets everyone and welcomes us in.
- He saved a special table for us and tells me not to look at the menu because he is going to surprise everyone. We all sit and the meal is great. Sergio, Lizzie, and I all order a glass of Grappa while Becky and Corina have some Sambuca. Our host brings out homemade pastries for the table.
- After dinner, we go back to our house and go to bed. We all can't wait to start another day together.

I have read many THAT DAY responses from students and clients over the years. There seems to be a common theme in the majority of them. The majority of activities and events on THAT DAY are simple in nature. Just like Tom's, both weekdays and weekends are spent doing simple but meaningful activities with those you love. There are rarely mentions of 10-bedroom mansions, expensive sports cars, designer clothes, C-level titles, seven-figure salaries, or levels of stardom. When we boil it down to how we define success, the THAT DAY exercise shows us that it all comes down to spending quality time with loved ones and doing what we love.

As you can read in Tom's version of THAT DAY, it is clear that he loves his family, cherishes his Italian culture, values his friendships, and loves to share love through food. In many cultures and families, food is a common love language. There is meaningful love in cooking, eating, sharing, and talking over a meal together that deepens our relationships and reassures us of the strong bond of love. For some families, this can be replaced with camping, playing music, playing sports, fishing, or another shared activity. Whatever it is for you, it is imperative to identify your favorite activities, validate their impact on your happiness, and document them. The THAT DAY exercise enables you to imagine the precise location and circumstance where you can experience maximum happiness.

Here is an interesting fact about Tom's version of THAT DAY. In 2019, he got to live out a portion of his THAT DAY. Tom and his wife Becky traveled to Italy and invited their son, daughter, and future daughter-in-law to spend the holidays with them in a beautiful rental house. While he is still working toward splitting his time between Italy and the U.S., Tom is consistent about experiencing portions of his THAT DAY in his current life, as he did over the holidays in 2019.

I invite you to design your own version of THAT DAY right now. It may be difficult for you to design the entire day. This is perfectly natural. I encourage you to start small. Pick a single activity you want to do or place you want to be, and design around it. Design at your own pace. However, do not procrastinate and put it off until the end of your busy day, or forget about THAT DAY. Even though it may take years to fully realize THAT DAY, we must keep visualizing it in our minds and hearts. That is the only way you'll remember to intentionally invest your time to live out small portions of THAT DAY every chance you get.

Every intentional practice of THAT DAY is a deposit you put toward maximizing your Life ROI.

> *Please use the following worksheet in The Life ROI Workbook to complete this step of the framework:* **STRATEGY I Strategic Design Worksheet**

Life ROI Framework: Plan

Identify

You have gone through gathering data, analyzing that data, creating strategic alignments, and designing what your ideal day-in-the-life looks like. Now it's time to put everything into a tactical plan so you can start intentionally living to increase your Life ROI.

Let's start with identifying which activities from THAT DAY you would like to start practicing now. Once you have a list of activities, please prioritize them based on the following criteria:

- How much time investment is required?
- Who else needs to be involved?
- How much financial investment is required?
- What other resources are required?
- How far in advance do you need to plan this activity?
- How feasible is it to practice this activity?

Now rate each activity on the following scale from 1 to 5:

1. Not feasible at all; the required amount of resources, investment, and planning in advance is beyond my current reality.

2. Requires a significant amount of resources, investment, and planning in advance

3. Requires a moderate amount of resources, investment, and planning in advance

4. Requires a minimum amount of resources, investment, and planning in advance

5. Very feasible; requires only a small amount of time investment

Start today with any activity that you rate as a 5. If you do not have any 5s, move down to the 4s and start pursuing one of those. Some of your activities that rate as a 5 may only require as little as 30 minutes to practice. Schedule those activities as soon as possible on your calendar (even today!) and start practicing a portion of THAT DAY it immediately.

Metrics

As an entrepreneur and business professor, I have an instinctual need to measure things to see if they are working or not. When I could not get the right metrics from the Point of Sales (POS) software I had purchased for MetroBoom, I built my own spreadsheets to track and measure what I needed as a business owner. The spreadsheets organically grew over time with new business requirements (things I wanted to measure and questions I could not find answers to). By the end, my spreadsheets were ginormous. Because it was for only one operation, these self-made, DIY system was not scalable or shareable, and that was ok. I learned a long time ago that no off-the-shelf solution can solve all of my problems. The best and most comprehensive solutions can only come from within. That doesn't mean that we need to create solutions on our own every time, locked in a vacuum. We always need outside perspective and expertise, but the ultimate strategy, design, and implementation for your needs has to come from within. Benchmarking is my go-to tool to identify, refine, and apply the best practices from various disciplines to create effective and comprehensive solutions. Also, as a startup entrepreneur, I am used to having to do more with less. I cannot always purchase systems and software whenever I need them. I have to be creative and scrappy to figure out other ways of doing things to minimize costs and get the solutions that I really need.

After my unsuccessful external research into Life ROI metrics and time tracking, I decided to get scrappy and do what I could with what I have. I had been using Google Calendar for years, so I started there. I scheduled my first intentional activity using the platform's provided fields. Here is my actual Google Calendar entry for my first intentional activity:

As you can see, I had only the minimum amount of details as this was my very first activity. This was a four-night, five-day family road trip to the Southwestern part of Colorado. My daughter was 12 years old, and this was our very first family vacation ever. This is concrete evidence of my "driven" attribute running wild in the liabilities column for 12 years. Shame on me.

At the time, there were no features in Google Calendar that would allow me to effectively track my intentional activities. However, I wanted to track and measure happiness as my first Life ROI criteria. Using my happiness equation, I first identified which activities generated happiness for me. If it generated happiness, I decided to tag the activity with the acronym "HP" (short for happiness) and search for "HP" at the end of every month to see how many events I had. I would then copy all the events tagged with "HP" and paste them into an Excel spreadsheet. I manually sorted and formatted the data to tally up the total amount of time I had intentionally invested in these activities. After the first month of tracking, I had my first Life ROI measurement for happiness. I was happy 17% of the time during the month of July 2017. This doesn't mean that 17% of happiness equates to 83% of misery, though. It just means that I was able to track 17% of my time when I intentionally invested in activities that made me happy. Some people have asked me if that is too low. I didn't know, as I never had a baseline or set an expectation for how much of my time should be invested in happiness. However, it was a start. For the remainder of 2017, I diligently scheduled intentional activities for happiness, and each month I manually tallied up the data in my spreadsheet. Here are the results from my happiness investment in 2017:

- July: 17%
- August: 10%
- September: 8%
- October: 14%
- November: 9%
- December: 6%
- Average over six-month period: 11%

During this six-month period, I experienced happiness 11% of the time.

While the size of the data set and length of the study were lacking, I was able to draw some anecdotal conclusions about the months with double-digit happiness percentages. In those three months, I had gone on road trips and weekend getaways. As a family, we loaded up the car and got out of Dodge. We left behind the everyday hustle and bustle. In the absence of social distractions and digital noise, we were able to spend quality time as a family. Based on this theory, I did my best to plan as many out-of-town trips for my family and I in 2018.

With six months under my belt, I set out to invest and track my happiness, satisfaction, and fulfillment throughout 2018. I also decided to add "#" in front of each activity tag. This allowed me to more accurately track and collect the right activities, because searching for tags without the "#" pulled other events and activities that had the same two-letter combination. These were my new tags:

- #HP: Happiness
- #FF: Fulfillment
- #SF: Satisfaction

I now had to identify components and create equations to measure fulfillment and satisfaction.

Fulfillment:

T = TIME

A = ACTIVITY

P = PEOPLE

O = OUTCOME

V = VALIDATION

F = FULFILLMENT

T (A + P + O + V) = FULFILLMENT

As mentioned in an earlier chapter, the key element in the fulfillment equation is the unsolicited validation of impact by those I serve. This means getting voluntary feedback from my students, clients, family, friends, colleagues, and community members. These validations would only count if they were provided voluntarily and were specific and detailed. "Good job" would not cut it.

Satisfaction:

T = TIME

A = ACTIVITY

O = OUTCOME

R = REWARD

F = SATISFACTION

$$T (A + O + R) = SATISFACTION$$

The critical element in the satisfaction equation is the exchange of fair-market compensation for my work. It is a purely functional transaction.

As I mentioned before, I was invited to teach and facilitate seminars at the Centre for Entrepreneurial Innovation and Research (CERI) in Perth, Australia. I met the founder, an amazing self-made American entrepreneur named Charlie Bass, at one of my sessions at Denver Startup Week. When I went to Perth, I was able to bring my family, including my mother, for 10 days of family vacation. Although the trip was long and grueling, my family and I thoroughly enjoyed every minute that we got to spend as a family down under. I got to witness expressions of exhilaration on the faces of my family. I loved every moment. I was genuinely happy.

After our wonderful trip to Australia, I vowed to continue my investment in happiness by going on more family trips. Therefore, my expectation for my investment in happiness for 2018 was high. Sadly, the average percentage of time I invested in happiness was 6% for 2018, a 5% drop from 2017 and net 45% decrease in my happiness. It would be very difficult for any business to survive after a 45% net loss from the previous year.

To be honest, I am not sure if I am the kind of person who would be happy with being happy most of the time. I think too much happiness would annoy me. As a cynical New Yorker, I need a healthy dose of misery and struggle in my life. However, 6% happiness didn't sit right with me, especially as a 45% loss compared to the previous year. I had to find the root cause for this significant drop. It didn't take me long to figure it out. The cause was the J.O.B. I had started in May 2018. Once the honeymoon period wore off as the president and supervisor who hired me were fired, that J.O.B. sucked out every ounce of my energy and passion. I felt like a caged hamster running in a toxic wheel of survival. As I discussed in an earlier chapter, I continually had to fight against leadership and colleagues who made shortcuts and compromises to meet the numbers, regardless of the harm they were causing to those we served. Fighting to keep my integrity intact at work was physically taxing and spiritually demoralizing. That J.O.B. also did not meet my fulfillment equation because my potential impact was trumped by the leadership's short-term needs to meet the numbers. Also, the new leadership dismissed and disrespected a written agreement to increase my salary after they fired the former president who hired me. It may have been legal, but it sure wasn't ethical. The experience of being cheated out $40,000 in my salary miserably failed to meet the threshold of the satisfaction equation. All three investments suffered during the seven months that I held that J.O.B. in 2018.

2018 Stats:

- #HP: Happiness = 6%
- #FF: Fulfillment = 3%
- #SF: Satisfaction = 2%

I exchanged control over my most valuable asset for steady paychecks. At the time, I needed to make the trade to better serve my family. I needed to provide stability for my family, so I was determined to stick it out. However, when I saw the average of 6% happiness at the end of the year, I knew this was not sustainable. I had been on this train before. I knew where this train was headed. I had to plan for some significant pivots in 2019.

One of the most positive outcomes from 2018 was meeting a young man with intelligence, hustle, and grit who was willing to build the web application I needed to track my Life ROI investments. I had been meeting with numerous technologists to design and build an application to track and measure my investments without having to manually process the data from Google Calendar to Excel spreadsheets. I had a difficult time finding the right person to work with. The work was too small for many technologists, and some of them wanted to make it more elaborate and complicated than it needed to be.

Dillon Pietsch intently listened to my needs and built the Life ROI time investment app from scratch. The app automatically pulls data from one's Google Calendar, and then sorts and tallies the tagged activities. Dillon and I both agreed that we would launch the beta version, which would only sync with my Google Calendar, to start. We wanted to test it and try to break it so we could discover all of the requirements needed from a business, user, and technical perspective. Dillon designed a dashboard that shows a quick overview of how I am doing with my investments at any given moment. This app gave me back the time I would have spent manually processing my calendar data into spreadsheets. I am so grateful that Dillon and I crossed paths when we did.

The year 2019 started in the same position as my 2018 had ended. I had not made any major changes in my life as I was still working on my strategies for 2019 and beyond. I spent what little free time I had to think and reflect on how my love, talent, and demands could align across clients, community, industries, and society. I utilized the Strategic Alignment diagram to validate my true passions, prioritize my professional paths, and align my passion, profession, and mission. During this time, I was able to ask myself some tough questions that I had never thought about before. Here are the some of the key questions I struggled to answer:

- What do I really love to do the most? Pick just one thing. Prioritize! Do not dilute!

- Is there a demand for what I love to do the most?

- If so, what are the known strategies and revenue channels to build a feasible, repeatable, and scalable business model?

- Based on my current resources and access to resources, what revenue-generating strategies can I start with?

- What are the tasks, deliverables, and timelines that I would need to implement these strategies?

- Will these decisions and activities provide satisfaction, fulfillment, and/or happiness?

At the end of March 2019, I reviewed my reports from the Life ROI time investment app. I was troubled by what I saw. As if my 6% happiness investment from 2018 wasn't bad enough, the first quarter of 2019 happiness investment was at 4.4%. My average percentage dropped 45% from 2017 to 2018, and the trend was continuing with another 27% drop in the first quarter of 2019. As I shared, the level of toxicity at my J.O.B. was rising and my integrity was being tested every day during this period. The amount of stress I was experiencing at work had a direct impact on my capacity to invest in my happiness. Some of you may wonder why I didn't intentionally invest more time into generating more happiness to combat and offset the stress from work. I tried. It made sense to do so, theoretically. However, when most of my time away from work was spent recovering and recharging, just to survive another day in the office, I simply had nothing left — not even for the intentional activities I knew would bring me happiness. This may not make much sense for some people, but it was true. I don't know how many of you have experienced this, but it can be quite draining and demoralizing. When April 3rd happened, it wasn't just my emotions that drove me to resign under duress. I had data to back-up my decision. It was quantifiable and unequivocal evidence that my happiness was disappearing out of my life at an alarming rate.

After leaving that toxic J.O.B., I began to intentionally invest in my happiness again and tried my best to bring more happiness into my life for the rest of 2019. That year's ending report showed a growth of 25%, increasing my average investment percentage from 4.4% in the first quarter to 5.5% by the end of the year. The growth may not seem drastic, and it wasn't to me either when I first saw it. However, it was a sobering reminder of how much intentional effort is required to generate meaningful and authentic happiness in our lives. It does not simply happen overnight because we wish for it or proclaim it to be true. It takes hard work, just like anything else worthwhile in life.

This is why we need relevant metrics. Strategy and implementation can be only as effective as the way by which progress is measured.

> *Please use the following worksheet in The Life ROI Workbook to complete this step of the framework:* **PLAN | Planning Worksheet**

Life ROI Framework: Implementation

By now, you have developed a meaningful tactical plan to carry out your Life ROI strategy, all based on data from you, your loved ones, and your life. The best plan in the world is only wishful thinking unless you execute that plan with commitment and intention.

The first step in implementation is to select your first intentional act of investment towards your Life ROI from the prioritized list of THAT DAY activities. Please treat this list differently than how you may have treated your New Year's resolutions. Also, do not treat this list like a 30-day challenge that your friend dragged you into on Facebook. This list requires consistent and intentional practice. You should not need any extrinsic motivations or reminders to practice these activities; you are doing them to experience authentic happiness. Remember, you don't have to do any of these activities. Nobody is making you do these activities. You are not doing these activities for anyone else. This is your list, created by you, for you. I do not wish to come across like a drill sergeant, but this is where excuses, procrastination, and fear must be put in check. Whatever or whoever was holding you back from pursuing what you desire also must be checked at the gate. I realize and embrace that there will be real-life circumstances, crises, and tragedies that may get in the way of practicing this list. That's expected and acceptable. However, I would like to encourage you to distinguish which factors truly need your attention and time versus which are just excuses, reasons to procrastinate, and fear. Only you will be able to discern the two. No one else will find out, but you will be the one paying the consequences. Keep your internal dialog open to recognize and isolate the excuses, procrastination, and fear from real-life issues. Argue against the voice of doubt, stagnation, and retrogression inside your head. Strip that voice of any power and dial it down, way down.

The second step is to intentionally schedule your first activity. Whether you use a digital calendar app or good ol' paper calendars, go ahead and schedule your first activity on your calendar. I sincerely hope your first activity is scheduled sooner rather than later so you can experience similar anticipation and excitement as I did when I scheduled my first intentional activity. I felt like a schoolboy counting down the days until Christmas.

If you are using a digital calendar app, please use the text fields provided by the app to record the details about the activity, e.g., date, time, duration, subject, location, invitee, notes, etc. If you recall my happiness equation from an earlier chapter, all of the equation's components with minor refinements are covered in the default text fields in most calendar apps. Please feel free to use my equation to start, or come up with your own process of recording the important details of your activities. I recommend:

- T = TIME
- A = ACTIVITY (record this in the subject field)
- P = PEOPLE (Use the invitee field if you want them to respond to the invite and have the activity on their calendar as well. If not, record this in the notes field)
- E = ENVIRONMENT (Record this in the location field)

As I mentioned in the section about measure, please create a hashtag for each activity that aligns with what you are seeking, e.g., satisfaction, fulfillment, happiness, joy, peace, etc. You may search for these hashtags in your calendar apps and generate the report manually in a spreadsheet like I did in the beginning of my Life ROI journey. If you are using Google Calendar, you are welcome to use the Life ROI app that Dillon built for me. If you are already using other calendar apps for work, you may set up a Google Calendar just to track your Life ROI activities. You can set up your account on the Life ROI app at: theliferoi.com

Now that you have successfully scheduled your first investment activity, the third step is to experience your authentic happiness. When you are immersed in your intentional activities, it is important to recognize the happiness you are experiencing in the moment. However, the instant you intellectually acknowledge what you are feeling, you are not actually experiencing happiness in that precise moment. It takes you away from being fully engaged in experiencing happiness. Therefore, you need to quickly return to the activity as soon as possible after you acknowledge your happiness. You can spend more time analyzing the activity, experience, and outcome later in the reflection and refinement phase of the framework. Nothing should take you away from genuinely enjoying happiness, especially any negative inner voices. If and when these voices chime in, please have a quick inner conversation to quiet those voices so you can return to experiencing your happiness.

I have found it useful to take pictures or short videos of my investment activities to capture those moments for documentation and reflection. The documentation helps me remember those moments and activities in the reflection and refinement phase. However, I make sure not to take too many pictures or too long of videos so I can stay fully engaged in the moment of happiness. Sadly, I have not always practiced this rule and have many regrets. For our 25th wedding anniversary, Alexis bought us tickets to a Billy Joel concert. When one of my favorite songs "New York State of Mind" came on, I wanted to capture it so I took my phone out to record it. Before I knew it, half of the song was over and I was still trying to keep a steady hand and zoom in for the perfect video frame. I realized I was missing out on enjoying my favorite song because I was too busy trying to document it. I was able to put my phone back inside my pocket and enjoy the second half of the song. Please remember that taking photos and videos is not as important as enjoying the moment itself.

Congratulations on your first Life ROI investment! I wish you many more intentional deposits in the upcoming days, weeks, months, and years ahead.

Life ROI Framework: Reflection & Refinement

Like many things in life, taking the first few steps are always the toughest part of the journey. Now that you have identified the activities that can provide experiences of happiness, scheduled them in your calendar, and followed through, how do you feel? Was it what you had expected? More? Or was it disappointing? What went right and what went wrong?

These intentional activities are too important to simply execute and move on from. In order to ensure you are making the right investments, you must take the time to reflect on these activities. The quick reflections while watching for the light to turn green or waiting to place your order at your favorite coffee shops may work. However, I recommend putting enough time on your schedule to reflect on a deeper level. You should find a calm and quiet place where you can reflect uninterrupted. Deep and honest reflection cannot be achieved if inner voices, external noise, and daily distractions are intruding every other minute. You must make room for recollection and analysis on how your investment paid off and how you may want to continue or refine your investment strategy. For me, when my schedule is full, I utilize local coffee shops for my reflection sessions. I discovered a while ago that while quiet places are often necessary for these sessions, for a city slicker like me, I cannot concentrate if it's absolutely silent. The mountain peaks or hidden hiking trails actually scare me. I am not at the top of the food chain in nature, and I cannot see if danger is coming like I am used to in a city environment. I can find my own peace and tranquility in a coffee shop amongst other people; they just need to be strangers so I don't have to interact with them. With my headphones on and my favorite tunes playing, my heartbeat slows down, my head clears, and I am able to dedicate 100% of my focus on the task at hand. Every now and then, I take short breaks to enjoy some people watching and sweet treats.

When I started this process, I reflected on a weekly basis to see how my investment performed. But with work, family, and life challenges, I decided it was more realistic to reflect on a monthly basis. Even still, sometimes it is challenging to maintain the monthly reflections. So, I pivoted and decided to reflect when I can schedule the time in advance, though I try my best to keep it at a monthly basis. If life happens and I have to miss my scheduled reflection sessions, I promise that I will not be too mad or hard on myself. Because the data is safely recorded on my Google Calendar and Life ROI app, I know I can review the dashboard anytime I want to. The point I want to emphasize here is that you should not treat your reflection time as another chore you have to complete. You have enough on your plate already, so cut yourself some slack when you have to attend to other things in life. Allow some flexibility to reschedule your reflection session.

For longer reflection sessions, I use my office at CU Denver's Business School so that I have full privacy in the luxury of my own space. When I need to wind down first before I start, I watch some Korean TV shows or catch up on Major League Soccer and English Premier League game highlights from the previous weekend. I also listen to ballads, R&B, blues, jazz or Ol'Blue Eyes to get my mind to slow down. Whether my reflection sessions are short or long, I consistently practice the following steps to ensure that I am gifting myself adequate time, head space, and heart space to take a look back on how I spent and invested the past weeks (or months):

- Review the intentional activities I scheduled on my calendar.

- Review the pictures I took during these activities on my phone, crosscheck these against my calendar to see if I missed scheduling any activities and adjust the time investment if the activities were cut short or extended.

- Review my social media posts to crosscheck against my calendar, see if I missed scheduling any activities, and adjust the time investment if the activities were cut short or extended.

- Once the calendar has been reconciled to ensure accuracy in my investment of intentional activities, I log onto the Life ROI app.

- Review the dashboard results for the intended time period to gauge any changes in the ROI of my happiness and other success attributes that I am tracking.

- Review the ROI performance for the calendar year to compare with the previous year and observe for any consistency or concerning changes as I experienced in 2018.

- Reflect on my top-performing activities and reassess my prioritized success attributes, if necessary. Make sure that I am effectively investing in the success attributes I prioritized based on what is going on in my life during that time period. Before I committed to writing this book, I didn't prioritize the time I would need to actually isolate myself, put my bottom firmly into a chair, and just write. After reflecting and addressing all of my excuses, I intentionally scheduled out and invested hours and days on my calendar to write. I did my best to stick to the planned schedule. It also alleviated the guilt and burden of not squeezing out time from the daily grind to write because I knew I had writing scheduled on my calendar.

- Reflect on all the activities and validate whether those activities actually delivered the desired outcome and contribution towards my success attributes. As we all know, there are so many factors that can ruin the perfect plan, external and internal. When an outcome didn't meet my expectation, I analyzed the circumstances around that activity to see whether uncontrollable external factors caused the discrepancy or if it was something I could control. When external factors caused or contributed to the undesired outcome, I remove them and schedule the same activity again to see if the outcome changes. When I caused or contributed to the undesired outcome, I evaluate my specific decisions and actions. I reflect on what I learned from the experience, and I schedule the same activity with a refined approach to seek a better outcome.

- For example, I planned a date night for Alexis and I to go watch a comedy show. We don't often get to spend quality time together, so I was really excited for the planned outing. Obviously, I had tagged #HP for this activity because spending quality time with my girl while enjoying good laughs sounded like a solid happiness activity. On our way to the comedy show, we got into an argument about halfway through the drive. There were multiple points in our conversation when I could have simply changed the subject or held back my thoughts from coming out of my mouth. But I didn't. Each time those options were available, I chose to continue the death march. We were not able to resolve the argument and make up before we walked into the theater. Needless to say, we sat through a very funny improv comedy show stewing in residual anger from the argument. Reflecting on this date night weeks later, I deleted the tag #HP from this activity before I ran my report on the Life ROI app. I was not happy during this activity and neither was Alexis. The desired outcome was not produced because I continued digging my own grave and didn't check my verbal diarrhea. I had control but I did not use it. What was the lesson learned? Save any topics that would potentially start an argument for another time. When the opportunity is available to check myself and pivot, take it. I strive to practice this valuable lesson on all date nights now.

- Reflect on my assumptions about my desired outcomes when those outcomes didn't produce the desired experience. Sometimes my assumptions are flawed. What I thought would make me happy or fulfilled simply didn't. The validation could only be gained after experiencing it and reflecting on it.

- I used to tag every activity I scheduled to spend time with my mom with #HP. My assumption was that spending time with my mom, regardless of the activity itself, would make me happy. Why wouldn't it? I love and respect my mom. We have so many things in common, and we can chat for hours. Reflecting on all the activities I schedule with my mom, I realized that some of them genuinely create happiness but not all do. Some create an experience of fulfillment, not happiness. As I explained in early chapter, fulfillment is not happiness. Fulfillment is delivering meaningful value and receiving unsolicited validation of the impact experienced from whom I serve. When the activities consisted of chores like grocery shopping, going to doctor appointments, or driving her to the hair salon, I felt like I was simply performing a son's duty. Activities that produce happiness included scenic drives, walks, delicious meals at my mom's favorite restaurants, my mom reading books while I work on my passion projects at coffee shops, surprise picnic lunches (preferably by a creek or a lake), and chatting on about how great my class or keynote event went while I savor every bite of my favorite meals mom prepared as she gazes a doting smile. I grew up with her love served in the bowls and plates that nourished me. I'd have a second serving and then a third to turn her gentle smile into a full-blown, Kool-Aid smile. Not only do I experience love from my mom's cooking, but it also heals me in times of trouble. My stress and worries melt away with each bite of her love. I genuinely experience healing and love when I am feasting on her culinary masterpieces.

- Instead of being disappointed with these unintended outcomes, I now schedule activities with my mom with #FF and #HP appropriately tagged so that my assumptions, expectations, and outcomes are all aligned.

During these reflection sessions, I discovered something unexpected. The activities I had been scheduling were designed to create happiness, which they did. However, when I thought about it on a deeper level and reflected on exactly what I was experiencing, I realized there were two different types of happiness. The type of happiness I was experiencing from these activities was an indirect happiness from making my family happy. All of the activities were chosen and designed to deliver happiness for my family and I collectively. My happiness was an ancillary by-product to my family's happiness.

The other type of happiness that I realized was absent from my Life ROI plan was the happiness I created for myself, by myself. These activities are scheduled without anyone else in mind and include activities that I want to do for myself in environments I want to be in. The resulting question of "What makes me happy?" was a lot tougher to answer than I expected. I don't think I am alone in this struggle; many parents, especially those who take care of both their elderly parents and their children, are not used to prioritizing themselves. For many of us, we are so used to taking care of everyone else's needs before our own. Thoughts of "self-care" or "my own happiness" do not readily exist in our minds.

After some inner discovery and evaluation, I was able to come up with one activity that I could do to make myself happy — by myself and for myself. I may be a complete outlier here but I love driving. Not necessarily in heavy traffic, but I love driving on the open road with my favorite tunes blasting and being alone with my thoughts. I immediately scheduled a driving session on my calendar and tagged it with #HP. I went for my first drive on I-25 around noon on a Thursday. There was no traffic on the highway at that time, as I had expected. I drove straight to Fort Collins and returned without stopping. The roundtrip took about two hours. My assumption was validated. Even reflecting back on those two hours of solo driving brought smile on my face. My thoughts wandered in many directions, reminiscing on the past, problem-solving current challenges, and visualizing my aspirations for the future. When sad ballads came up on my playlist, the lyrics would trigger memories of stressful times I had endured. I got emotional. I cried, out loud sometimes. I felt safe expressing my raw emotions in the safety and the privacy of my own car while traveling 65 miles an hour. I didn't have to worry about people gawking. "My Way" by Frank Sinatra not only got me teary eyed as I imagined facing my own final curtain, but I also felt inspired to live the rest of my life with intention so that I can confidently go out with too few regrets to even mention.

After a good venting session with a few special songs that deeply move me, I reflected on all that I have gone through. How I survived, hustled, and thrived through the challenges I have faced. A calm inner voice chimed in, "You will get through whatever you are struggling with right now. You did it before, many times. You can and will do it again."

This was not my ego filling my head with loud, conceited thoughts but rather stating logical fact based on actual experiences and reassuring me of my earned confidence. I have been intentionally engaging this inner whisper of thunder when I need to be at my best.

I experienced genuine happiness in each driving session. Sometimes, I would pull over for a sandwich at a rest stop. It made me feel like I was on a road trip. I love traveling and these driving sessions produced the endorphins I get from traveling. It was a poor man's version of traveling but it did the job. I was happy.

Another realization that enabled me to refine my investment plan was my need for longer reflection sessions. Since I began my work on Life ROI and writing this book, I realized some of my work could not be completed effectively or efficiently in two- or three-hour increments. I needed longer sessions to completely immerse myself in the tasks at hand without interruptions. This need was validated when I read *Deep Work* by Cal Newport. I instantly resonated with Newport's hypothesis on deep work: "The ability to perform deep work is becoming increasingly valuable in our economy. As a consequence, the few who cultivate this skill, and then make it the core of their working life, will thrive."[3]

Then I read about a person I have never met but who has been in my life since I moved to the U.S. When people read my name, the majority of them treat the "J" as silent and pronounce my name as "Young." I mainly credit Carl Jung for this mispronunciation of my name. I would find another connection with Carl Jung in *Deep Work*:

Carl Jung kept a busy schedule with his lectures and counseling practice in Zurich. In the Swiss canton of St. Gallen, near the northern banks of Lake Zurich, is a village named Bollingen. In 1922, Jung built a basic two-story stone house he called the Tower. Jung retreated to Bollingen, not to escape his professional life, but instead to advance it.

When Carl Jung wanted to revolutionize the field of psychiatry, he built a retreat in the woods. Jung's Bollingen Tower became a place where he could maintain his ability to think deeply and then apply the skill to produce work of such stunning originality that it changed the world. Build our own personal Bollingen Tower to cultivate an ability to produce real value in an increasingly distracted world; and to recognize a truth embraced by the most productive and important personalities of generations past: A deep life is a good life. [4]

The book describes four different philosophies to guide the practice of deep work. Ironically, Carl Jung's practice of deep work resonated with me the most.

---

[3] Cal Newport, *Deep Work: Rules for Focused Success in a Distracted World* (London: Piatkus, 2016), page 14

[4] Newport, *Deep Work*, page 1, 18

Unlike the Jung in Bollingen back in 1922, this Jung in Colorado in 2019 cannot afford to build a two-story stone house. However, I had to figure out how I can practice intentional deep work, away from daily life's responsibilities and distractions, to focus on my passion projects for a few days. I didn't need a week-long, luxurious retreat. What I needed was a quick reset, an intentional isolation to reflect, do some deep thinking, and focus on completing prioritized tasks over a period of two or three days. All I needed was the basic necessities to work, sleep, eat, and wash up — no pampering, no frills.

I shared the challenges I was facing and my idea for a reset with Alexis. As always, she was very supportive of my idea and gave me her blessings. My first reset was at a historic hotel in Estes Park. I have always loved Estes Park, and this hotel was running a special deal I could not pass up. I booked a modest studio unit for three nights at a very reasonable rate. My mom packed me a cooler full of her love-filled meals, which was more than enough food for my stay. As always, she didn't want her boy to get hungry. I spent three nights and days reflecting, thinking, and working. I actually wrote the first 40 pages of this book during this reset. I was able to reach deeper levels of reflection and thinking than I could before. The intentional isolation, commitment to focus, and responsibility of my family's sacrifice for me be away for few days were catalysts for the reset's success. In the next few months, I went on two more resets with the singular focus of finishing this book. I found even more modest accommodations at lower rates in the town of Lyons, Colorado. Of course, the cooler with my mom's love-stuffed meals came with me to both resets.

These resets were not only productive for my prioritized tasks but they were also transformational and essential for the deeper levels of reflections I wanted to reach. Being alone and choosing to sit with my feelings and thoughts for as long as I needed to allowed me to create the head space and heart space to gain new perspectives. All the dots were connecting in my head at a lightning speed and with superb clarity. Those gloomy clouds of doubt, fear, and distractions were giving way to beams of conviction, brightening the path before me. My inner whisper of thunder was recharging with authentic confidence the whole time. As I drove back home from each reset, I realized these sessions were healing my mind, heart, body, and soul.

For some, these two- or three-day resets may be too short. You may benefit more from longer retreats, perhaps over a week or two. I encourage you to go on at least one retreat if you can afford it. For budget-conscious and time-constrained folks like me, I strongly recommend taking short, weekend resets. I sincerely hope you will find these shorter resets as productive, cathartic, and healing as I have.

Regardless of the type and length of your reset and reflection sessions, the most important component is the intentional investment of your time to fulfill your intrinsic need for deep work and reflection. Find what works best for you given your personality, limitations, and circumstances. Commit to scheduling the activity on your calendar. Experience and enjoy it with your mind and heart wide open. Reflect on it, and analyze what you need to repeat and what you need to refine. Schedule your next one, experience, reflect, and refine. Then rinse and repeat, perfecting the practice of resetting as you go.

Wishing You a Good Journey

I have been blessed to consult for corporate, nonprofit, and individual clients in various industries and sizes over the past 20 years. I have also immensely enjoyed teaching students and speaking in front of audiences of diverse backgrounds on various subjects, both within the U.S. and abroad. Whether I am consulting, teaching, or speaking, my focus is always to serve my constituents to the best of my abilities as a Sherpa.

My philosophy is to guide my clients, students, and audience members through my Life ROI framework so that they can own their own path and achieve their individual definition of success. In the big picture of life, I am on the journey with those I serve to think, feel, collaborate, struggle, and achieve together. Their success is my success, and vice versa. From time to time, I would lead from the front to shed light on the unknowns, pointing out pitfalls, risks, possible routes, and critical reflections. Sometimes I would walk side-by-side with them as a peer on this crazy journey called life. I lend my shoulder for them to lean and cry on. I also offer to carry their burden filled backpacks for a short time when they need it on harrowing trails. I would also walk behind them sometimes to help push them forward and whisper thunder in their sails to bolster their confidence. I want them to feel supported and grounded, knowing that someone has their back. While common titles like consultant, strategist, coach, advisor, professor, and speaker appropriately describe what I functionally do, I embrace the title, philosophy, and approach of a Sherpa to describe who I am, as well as how and why I do what I do.

My approach to writing this book was no different. I wanted to write this book from the perspective of a Sherpa. Each person reading this book is on their own individual path. No two paths are the same. As I share the struggles and key learnings from my own journey in this book through the Life ROI framework, it is not meant to be used as a strict process or protocol to follow, step by step. Rather, it is a framework, by its own definition, a work of constructed frames with openings to be filled by its implementer. You get to fill in the blanks with your own learnings, reflections, strategies, and needs. This book should be used as a map to guide you on your journey. This map does not lay out the best route for you to follow. This map provides high-level directional guidance for you to consider, but you ultimately have to discover and forge your own path forward. It is also up to you to identify and set up points of interest, rest stops, watering holes, and sanctuaries. You have absolute control over when and how you utilize them to gain sustenance, nourishment, rest, and inspiration to thrive on your journey. This book and I will be at your side to guide and support you. But only you can own your journey. Invest with intent and increase your Life ROI with purpose. The true answers to what you are seeking are always within you. Your life's purpose is whispering from within. Listen...

Acknowledgments

I dedicate this book to those who fill my heart with love, passion, and inspiration every day.

My mom is my North Star. She gave me life and so much more. She embodies the pinnacle of love, compassion, grit, passion, and drive. My mom didn't tell me what to do. She showed me. She led through her actions. She modeled every lesson I have ever learned from her. My mom survived hardships I can't even imagine from my privileged, Gen Xer perspective. She gritted through the challenges and thrived in ways that seem fictional. Standing tall at 5 feet and barely breaking triple digits on the scale, my mom possesses the wisdom and strength that would cripple the most established intellects and the strongest giants. Her calm demeanor and petite frame should not to be mistaken as weaknesses for she is truly a force to reckon with. I always felt her love growing up. I witnessed her love through her sacrifices as I grew older. I am still consuming her love in every meal she prepares. My mom's love language is food and I am fluent in it. We have a lot of things in common, physically, intellectually, and emotionally. I am blessed. I am grateful. Through our conversations, I get to learn, grow, and validate my own truth. In times of trouble, I look up to her to remind myself that I have inherited her gene for grit, and I regain the strength to push forward. In times of joy, I can't wait to share it with her to see the smile of pride on her face. I like to think that her smile is proof that her sacrifices were meaningful and worthwhile. I love her. I respect her. I am proud to be her son.

엄마,
엄마는 제마음속에 계신 북극성이란것 아시죠? 엄마 아들로 태어난 제가 얼마나 축복받은 녀석이란것 항상 감사하게 생각합니다. 이 축복받은 인생을 그동안 엄마의 희생과 고생에 보답할수있게 최선을 다해 보람되게 살겠습니다. 사랑합니다. 존경합니다. 엄마 아들이란게 자랑스럽습니다. 건강하게 오래 오래 저희곁에서 밝은 북극성이 되어주십시요.

Alexis and I got married when we were barely 23 years old. As two young and naive newlyweds, the odds were stacked against us on so many levels. We spent the past 25 years growing up together and shaping each other into the people we are today. We have been through so much, and we stand tall today because we are together. I do not think I would have been able to get through it all if I hadn't had Alexis's trust and unyielding support. In times of trouble, she doubled down and stood by my side. In times of joy, she elevated it to a higher level, a level that would have been unreachable on my own. Alexis blessed me with two loving, caring, intelligent, and gorgeous children. She is a great partner in raising our kids to become compassionate and contributing human beings.

Alexis,

I know how tough it is to be married to someone like me. I also know that it is a lot easier for me to be married to you. I am grateful. Thank you for grounding me and preventing my entrepreneurial ADHD from chasing shiny, floating objects over the cliff. I had written a short speech for the business plan competition back in 2004, just in case I would win. When I was awarded the first-place award, I was excited to share how I felt about you in public and to acknowledge all of the love, support, and sacrifices you had made for me. Unfortunately, they never allotted me the time at the podium to deliver my speech. So, 16 years later, I get to do it in my first book. Knowing I have your love and support, I feel 10 feet tall. With you by my side, I feel the strength and confidence to conquer anything in my path. I cherish my life with you. When I face my final curtain, it is your hand I want to hold. It is your lovely face I want to look into as I thank you for a life that was full. I thank you. I adore you. I love you!

In the Korean culture, it is the oldest sibling's duty to take care of the younger ones. As the older brother, I did all I could to take care of my sister, especially after I realized how horrible I had been to her when we were younger. I had a lot to make up for. Reflecting on our relationship, I realized my sister has been more like an older sister to me over the years. Just like our mom, she let her actions do the talking. Quietly but abundantly, my sister cared for me with love and support. Her talent for design, relentless work ethic, and pragmatic approach immensely helped me with starting and operating MetroBoom. Even though she is now thousands of miles away in NYC, she cares for our mom in ways that I cannot. She is the cool aunt who knows just how to properly spoil her niece and nephew. My kids have an additional source for unconditional love in my sister. They are blessed, just like I am.

연정아,
오빠는 난데 너는 항상 나한테 누나 처럼 뒤에서 조용히 나를 아껴주고 돌봐줬어. 철없을땐 아무생각없이 너에게 상처주를 주곤했지. 많이 미안하다. 나에게 누나같은 동생이 있다는것이 너무 고마워. 앞으로 항상 네곁에서 지켜주고 돌봐줄게. 사랑한다 연정아!

Maddie is my princess. She blessed me with so many wonderful first-time experiences as a father. I see some of my mom and sister in her as she is reserved with her words but her actions are loud and powerful. Fortunately for her, Maddie is a carbon copy of Alexis, simply gorgeous! She has yet to discover all the reasons she has to be confident and strong. I am so excited for the day when she does because she will be a force to reckon with, regardless of what she is doing and where she is.

Maddie,

I will strive to be the dad you want and need me to be. While my stern tone and RMF may inadvertently hurt your feelings, please know that my intentions could not be more opposite. I look forward to watching you grow up to become the compassionate, intelligent, powerful, and beautiful woman you are destined to be. I will always have your back, my princess. Thank you for being my daughter. I love you!

Mateo turned our world upside down for the better when he was born. He smiled when he was just a few months old, a sneak peek into his kind, loving, and compassionate nature. He makes friends everywhere he goes, which he got from Alexis. I was blown away when I witnessed Mateo practicing empathy towards Maddie at the ample age of 5, as Alexis and I had not explicitly taught him anything about empathy. He must have inherited that from my mom.

Mateo,

Although you are my son, you teach and inspire me to become a better man. You naturally possess qualities that I strive for. I am in awe of your innate connection to your emotions and ability to make people happy. I will strive to be the dad you want and need me to be. Watching you become a compassionate, intelligent, dynamic, and handsome man will be simply delightful. I will always have your back, buddy. Thank you for being my son. I love you!

Special thanks to my friends who have been there to support me through thick and thin. I am truly blessed to have them in my life.

Doug Thielen,

You were a client first, a close friend later, then a savior. I am forever grateful to you for saving my life on that fateful day in 2016. I would not be here today if it wasn't for you. This book and my work in Life ROI would not have been possible if it wasn't for you. I appreciate you, Doug.

Emerson Bonilla,

You always had my back, through thick and thin. No matter how difficult or dirty the task was, you were there, even before I had to ask. You are a true friend. Thank you for your loyal friendship. I appreciate you, Emerson.

Jason Regier,

You inspire me on so many levels. Your humility is contagious. I appreciate your confidence in me and for calling me out when I need a wake-up call. Thank you for pushing me forward. I appreciate you, Jason.

Karen Hertz,

You balance out my bitter cynicism and RMF with your sunshiny personality and smile. Your trust in me and support saved me from the valley of hardship. Thank you. I appreciate you, Karen

Madhavan Parthasarthy (MP),

You have been there for me through the peaks and valleys of my journey, always extending your hand as a mentor and friend. You opened doors and kept them open for me. Thank you for taking me under your wing. I appreciate you, MP.

Bryan Van Dyke,

You have taught me the definition of servant leadership through your actions. Your friendship and support got me through some of the toughest times in my life. You are the older brother I wished I had. I appreciate you, Bryan.

Patrick Brown,

Whether it was a sandwich to nourish me or holding me accountable to accomplish what I set out to do, you have always been there to keep me going. I appreciate you, Patrick.

Alison Spada,

You have taught me patience and unyielding friendship. It has been an honor be your older brother from another mother. We have been through a lot, and we have survived it all. I look forward to supporting each other through whatever life has in store. I appreciate you, Al.

Brenda Henry,

As the tough catcher from the Bronx protecting the plate to the passionate Ph.D. protecting the wellbeing of the public, you motivate me to do better. You always kept it real. You help me stay true. I appreciate you, Brenda.

Domingo Tanco,

For the past 30 years, you have been a loyal friend, through and through. You were next to me clubbing during high school, stood by my side on my wedding day, and you are the first to text me happy birthday every year. I know you have my back and I got yours. I appreciate you, Ming!

Gimena Sanchez-Garzoli,

You were the first friend who gave me a hug at LaGuardia. I remember how comforting it was for this awkward and insecure immigrant boy. I am grateful of our friendship and how we can always pick up where we left off, regardless of how much time has passed. I appreciate you, Gimena.

To the inaugural cohort of my Life ROI seminar:

Thank you for taking the brave step to invest six weeks of your life in my very first Life ROI seminar. I have learned so much from your struggles, triumphs, and reflections. I am honored to be a small part of your journey, and my journey has been elevated by each of you.

I would like to applaud each of you for practicing your vulnerability and bravery to own your journey and increase your Life ROI. It was a pleasure to serve you.

I appreciate you, Sergio.

I appreciate you, Tom (especially for sharing your story of THAT DAY in this book).

I appreciate you, Kate.

I appreciate you, Tanner.

I appreciate you, Jason.

I appreciate you, Leah.

I appreciate you, Tricia.

I appreciate you, Rob.

I appreciate you, J.

About Jung

Jung has over 20 years of consulting experience in design, branding, marketing, user experience, strategy, and business development. He also has over 15 years of experience as a start-up entrepreneur in all facets of entrepreneurship from funding to operations.

Leveraging his experience from consulting and his passion for strategy and entrepreneurship, Jung has built a unique platform of services. He provides a full suite of consulting and advisory services in entrepreneurship, strategy, culture, equity, communication, leadership, marketing, and branding to corporate, start-up and non-profit clients. Jung also delivers key notes, seminars and facilitates workshops on the subjects of corporate/personal branding, professional/personal development, leadership, Life ROI, entrepreneurship, value, culture, equity, inclusion, diversity, and Asian-American empowerment.

As an adjunct professor at University of Colorado Denver, Jung teaches marketing, entrepreneurship, leadership, and personal branding for the Professional MBA, 1-Year MBA, and Executive MBA programs. Jung also serves as an advisory council member and entrepreneur in residence at the Jake Jabs Center for Entrepreneurship at University of Colorado Denver.

Jung currently lives in Lakewood, Colorado with Alexis, Madison, Mateo, and his mom lives just five minutes away from him.

To learn more about Jung, please visit: www.jungpark.me

Made in the USA
Coppell, TX
11 August 2020